D1567180

American Miniature
Case Art

American Miniature Case Art

Floyd and Marion Rinhart

South Brunswick and New York: A. S. Barnes and Company

London: Thomas Yoseloff Ltd

© 1969 by A. S. Barnes and Co., Inc.

Library of Congress Catalogue Card Number: 68–27207

A. S. Barnes and Co., Inc.
Cranbury, New Jersey 08512

Thomas Yoseloff Ltd
108 New Bond Street
London W. 1, England

SBN 498–06867–6

Printed in the United States of America

Contents

List of Illustrations

List of Plates

Introduction

The miniature case, a container used to hold portraits and scenes of America shortly after the advent of photography in 1839, is a little known art craft of the nineteenth century. During its zenith period, the miniature case became one of the important personal art forms to enter the home. Almost every dwelling in the mid-nineteenth century, rich or poor, had one or more of these decorative objects proudly displayed for intimate viewing.

Portraits on early silvered-copper plates called daguerreotypes, and later on glass, tin, and paper, were considered by Americans during the pioneer era of photography to be precious heirlooms—ones suitable for posterity. The necessity to preserve the new photographic art from the elements had spawned a new industry—cases in miniature made especially for photographs.

As collectors of pioneer photography, we have had an opportunity to study and view a very large number of miniature cases, both those of wood-frame construction covered with leather, paper, or cloth, and those made of a plastic composition. We feel that the scenes and designs in relief depicted on case covers during the era of the miniature case reflect the thoughts and feelings of an age—an outpouring of artistic talent that has generally remained unseen for a century.

Since the craft and art of the miniature case has not had a previous historian, except in a brief outline form, our undertaking has been one of considerable research. Contemporary books of the mid-nineteenth century were consulted, a persistent search through United States Letter Patent records was undertaken, a bit of information was gathered here and there from old directories and newspapers—all helped to piece together a history of the miniature case. Research proved especially difficult because manufacturers' records have long since disappeared and only fragments remain.

We, the authors, alone must be held responsible for any errors on the following pages, and would welcome any criticism or new knowledge on the subject from those interested; additional material must come from the many existing collections which are now scattered far and wide. Much erroneous information has existed in regard to miniature case history and very often popular notions have no bearing on facts and evidence.

We have used special lighting effects to photograph the miniature cases illustrated in this book in order to highlight the intricately formed designs; subject treatment stands out more clearly through this method. We have provided titles for many of the plates and have classified designs in general categories whenever possible. Because geometric forms were difficult to catalog, we decided to separate them into groups according to their predominant shapes. Judgments on the rarity of cases found in "Notes on Plates" are based only on our own observations and other contemporary opinions.

We are indebted to many persons for help in locating needed materials both for the text and illustrations. Dr. Philip W. Bishop, Chairman, Arts and Manufactures, Smithsonian Institution, Washington, D. C., allowed us the use of his notes on Scovill Manufacturing Co. business papers which were important to the text. Miss Josephine Cobb, Specialist of Iconography, National Archives, Washington, D. C., generously suggested several fruitful avenues of research and also allowed us to photograph some needed cases from her own collection. Mr. J. Harry Du Bois of Watchung, New Jersey, an internationally known figure in the plastics industry, sent us his own research materials and writings and allowed us to use his photographs. He also sent important cases to be photographed. We are grateful to The New York Historical Society and Dr. James J. Heslin, Director, for sending needed photographs of interesting cases from the society's fine case collection. The Pro-Phy-Lac-Tic Brush Company, Florence, Massachusetts, aided our project by sending photographs and other informative material.

The Frick Art Reference Library; The Metropolitan Museum of Art; Library of Congress; The New Haven Free Public Library, New Haven, Connecticut, and Margaret C. Dilzer of their Reference Department, were helpful in furnishing historical data. We would like to thank Mrs. Beula Butts, Librarian of Melbourne Public Library, Melbourne, Florida, for obtaining needed reference books.

We are deeply indebted to the following case collectors for listing designs and sending us cases to be photographed for this book: Mrs. Lucille Boss, Brooklyn, New York; Mr. Jack T. Ericson, Wisconsin Historical Society, Madison, Wisconsin; Mr. Emerick J. Hanzl, Clifton, New Jersey; Mr. Frederick Reehl, Vero Beach, Florida; Mrs. Janie Wright, Jane's Antiques, Richmond, Virginia; Mr. Norman Mintz and Mr. Morris Weiss of Time-Out Antiques, New York City.

The late Mrs. Dorothy Ross, Deerfield Beach, Florida, read the manuscript and offered many valuable improvements. Mr. George G. Hutchinson, chairman, division of English, Mills College of Education, New York City, edited the manuscript and contributed important suggestions. We are indebted to Mrs. Maude Cottrell, Point Pleasant, New Jersey for helping to classify case designs.

FLOYD and MARION RINHART

American Miniature
Case Art

PART I

Miniature Cases: History and Art

1
The Making of a Miniature Case

The miniature case was not a new idea in 1839; for years it had been used by artists to enclose small portraits. However, it was in this year that a new use was found for the leather-covered case. It would also, henceforth, be used to hold the pictures produced by the newly perfected photographic art. From 1840 onward, the art craft of casemaking suddenly funnelled into a rapidly expanding industry. Millions of these small cases in varying sizes were produced in the 1840-1850 period and well into the 1860's. At its zenith, the miniature case provided Americans, rich or poor, with an opportunity to enhance their likenesses from the camera's lens. The daguerreian artists termed it "an everlasting keepsake."[1]

European photographers of the day, with the exception of the English, did not follow this use of the traditional art case to enclose their photographs but framed them on mats under glass. So it was that placing photographs in the miniature case was peculiarly an American adaptation. Later, the widespread popularity of paper photographs and the prevalence of wartime conditions—inferior craftsmanship and materials, the use of the small case fell into obsolescence.

On September 30, 1839, the New York *Morning Herald,* describing the first public display of the newly invented photographic process, wrote, "It is the first time that the rays of the sun were ever caught on this continent, and imprisoned in their glory and beauty, in a morocco case with golden clasps." The morocco case mentioned was probably made originally for a miniature painting because, the newspaper went on to explain, the photographic plate was equal in size to a miniature painting. The new art of photography quickly adopted the same style case for its own use.

The history of the miniature case had been an interesting one before that September day of 1839. Ever since 1795 there had been a gradual increase in the size of miniature paintings, and the popular style of their cases had slowly changed from an oval to a rectangular shape.[2] The rectangular miniature case had an advantage—it could stand upright for easy placement on a desk or mantel for frequent viewing. In contrast, the oval shape had been hung on the wall or, in a small size, worn on the person. By 1840 general size proportion for the rectangular case was a ratio of four-fifths of an inch in width to each inch in length. In thickness, it was generally five-eights of an inch.[3] There were fractional variations, however, not only in the thickness, but the length and width, depending on the individual casemaker.

To the miniature casemaker of 1840 a new world of expansion had opened; but sharp competition was also on the horizon, in the form of new efficient production methods of casemaking (*see* Fig. 1). Jewel casemakers, case suppliers for surgical instruments, wood box manufacturers, and those in other related fields all joined the rush to supply the new demand created by the daguerreian artists.

Basic materials for the making of a miniature case were

The wood used by most casemakers was a soft native pine, although in 1847 William Shew, Boston casemaker, turned out a number of cases using mahogany. The grade of wood used varied from a clear vertical grain to lower grades, which included knots (*see* Figs. 2 and 3). Woodworking skills varied with individual makers, ranging from neatly made cases to shoddy ones. During the Civil War period poorly made cases were the rule rather than the exception.

The wooden framework, having passed through the action of various saws, gouges and grinding wheels, a total of twenty different millwork manipulations, was now ready for the exterior finish. The first step was the application of the "tops," as they were called, which were made from the finest leather skivers, usually of paper-thin sheepskin.[6] To obtain embossed "tops," the casemaker relied on concerns which specialized in making embossed articles for a custom trade, although in some instances they did their own stamping. The embossed designs on leather, cardboard, or paper "tops" were made by

Fig. 1. A typical case of the 1839–1840 era. The covering was a single piece of embossed leather. In the early 1840's, a five-piece leather method made the case (shown above) obsolete.

wood for the frame, leather and metal fasteners for the exterior; for the inside—cotton, cardboard, silk or velvet, glass, and brass fittings were needed.[4] Ten pieces of shaped wood, when fitted together and glued, formed the skeleton framework of the top and bottom parts of the case (*see* Fig. 2). Usually the shape of top and bottom was identical; however, sometimes the cover was elliptical, while the bottom was rectangular in form, with the thickness of the wood beveled to a feathered edge.at the rail (side rim). In the early 1850's, an innovation of laminated wood covers and bottoms increased the number of wood parts to fourteen (*see* Fig. 3). This method was introduced to overcome the wood's tendency to twist and warp.[5] About the same time, rail joints changed from a 45-degree miter cut to a mortised joint (*see* Figs. 2 and 3).

Fig. 2. Typical wood-frame construction in the 1840's, interior view. The illustration shows the rail separated from the solid wood.

Fig. 3. Typical wood-frame construction in the 1850's, exterior view. The illustration shows the cross-grain reinforcing on each surface end of the case cover.

a die press. A brass cylinder die, cut with raised design figures, was most generally used, although other adaptable materials were sometimes used to make the die. The making of the die for embossing was a separate industrial art. The embossed or plain tops were cut to proper size to cover the case surface parts (*see* Fig. 4). They were secured by placing them on the wet glue which was on the wood surface and were then repeatedly brushed with a blunt rubber stick until the glue had set, taking care that the embossings were not injured.[7] It was not until 1854 that this laborious gluing process was accelerated and improved through the invention of Henry T. Anthony's press for covering miniature cases (*see* Fig. 5).

The tops, after gluing, were always a little larger than the wood surface. The leather parts on their four-perimeter edges were trimmed back to the size of the surface and shaved with such skill as to leave a feathered edge (*see* Fig. 4). Thus, the top was ready to accommodate the "strip" which was a piece of high quality very thin leather. It was long enough and wide enough to cover the two side rails, the front rail, and be returned a short distance on either end of the back rail and at the same time it covered the exposed rail on the inside of the case (*see* Figs. 2 and 4 for rail parts to be covered). The leather was pared to a feathered margin on the exterior long edge so that when glued to the fine edge of the "top," it would make an almost imperceptible joint.

To complete the leather work on the case exterior, a strip

Fig. 4. The embossed leather "tops" were glued directly to the sanded wood as illustrated here.

Fig. 5. Henry T. Anthony's press was the first patented invention aimed at increasing production of the miniature case. U.S. Patent record is shown above. The press eliminated hand labor to glue embossed "tops" on miniature cases.

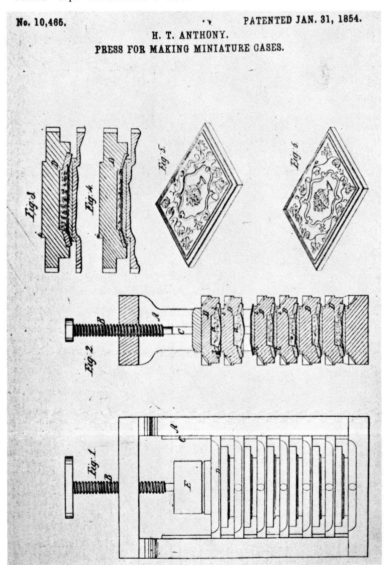

No. 10,465.   PATENTED JAN. 31, 1854.

H. T. ANTHONY.

PRESS FOR MAKING MINIATURE CASES.

of slightly heavier leather, called the "inside-outside back," was put in place on both the inside and the outside rear rails of the case; this formed the case's hinge and concealed the exterior portion of wood left uncovered by the strip and at the same time covered the rear rail which was the center part of the case when opened.[8] Many casemakers, using their fingernails, creased the rail edges of the finished strip to create sharp lines.[9] Later, with the advent of paper, cardboard, and cloth-covered cases, the "inside-outside back" was made from cloth instead of leather and applied in the same manner. Very few leather cases used the standard small brass hinges so familiar with the plastic case. With the application of a leather or cloth hinge, the components became a box with both the cover and bottom in place and joined.

case. The "eye" was fashioned from a thin malleable brass strip one-eighth inch in width, three-quarters in length, and pointed at both ends. The brass strip was then folded in the shape of a hairpin. The pointed ends were pressed together and passed through a pre-drilled hole in the front rail of the case's cover, leaving only the fashioned eye visible on the exterior (see Figs. 2 and 3). The prongs were bent on the inside of the rail in opposite directions to secure the eye. A thin coat of transparent varnish was then applied for a finished case exterior.[10]

The inside furnishings that were added after the exterior was complete were generally uniform for most miniature cases, varying only in minor details. The term "trimmed" was used

Fig. 6. The embossing on the miniature case shown here was designed by B. C. True, Albany, N. Y., *circa* 1842.

Fig. 7. Casemakers often embossed the photographer's name and address on the velvet pad in the case interior at no extra charge, except for the initial die.

Two steps were now required to complete the exterior—attaching the metal fasteners and applying a coat of varnish. The miniature case—other than those of plastic composition or the few leather or papier-mâché cases with snap fasteners—was held closed by a simple hook and eye. Often, two fastenings were used to prevent warping. The tiny hook, three-quarters of an inch long, was ornamented cast brass; it was riveted fast through the front rail of the bottom part of the by casemakers to describe the placement of the interior finished parts. The inside cover was completed first by attaching a cloth-covered pad, usually of embossed velvet, or plain silk in solid colors of red, or blue, or purple, and occasionally green (see Fig. 7). The cloth was cut a quarter of an inch larger than a piece of cardboard over which the fabric was folded to give it shape and rigidity; a small flat wad of cotton was often placed between the cloth and cardboard to create a pillow effect. The assembly and placing of the pad was done by hand; the four edges of the cloth were carefully glued to the rear of the cardboard, taking care to prevent staining of the material. The next step was to put glue on the cardboard side of the pad; it was then placed on the inside cover of the case. However, a process which eliminated some of the hand pad-work, through the use of a press machine, was patented by Henry T. Anthony and Frank Phoebus on May 23, 1854 (U. S. Patent 10,953).

The inside bottom part of the case intended to hold the picture was finished last. A piece of paper, usually white, was trimmed to proper size (sometimes with the makers' name, see Fig. 14) and glued to the case bottom.[11] The next step was to glue a narrow strip of velvet-covered cardboard, generally one-sixteenth of an inch in thickness by five-sixteenth of an inch in width, around the inside perimeter of the case bottom. The purpose was twofold; it made a frame of velvet to enhance the photographer's art and it insured a snug fit so that the photographic unit (picture, mat, glass and protector) would not fall out when handled (see Fig. 11 for photographic unit in place).

In displaying early photography, regardless of whether the image was on metal or glass, two components, a mat and glass were needed to protect and enhance the picture—if a "protector" was used, the necessary parts increased to three.

A "mat" was used to embellish portraits and scenes, to provide a border, and to accentuate the image. Mats were formed from sheet-brass and were known variously as "common," "fire-gilt," "engraved," or "stamped"; differences consisted in the value of the metal or the cost and style of finishing.[12] The mats were made with a powerful steam press which first cut the "blanks" (without the center shape removed), and then another press cutter stamped out the shaped opening (see Fig. 8). Sometimes acids were applied to the surface of the mat so that the appearance would be "frosted" or "marked," but generally a pebble or sand finish was stamped on the brass. The inside of the opening was chamfered and burnished, and finally the mat lacquered.[13] The first mat design was patented by Hiram W. Hayden (U. S. Design Patent 733) and issued on October 9, 1855; it was manufactured by Holmes, Booth and Hayden of New York City (see Fig. 9).

The surface of the photograph was protected by a piece of clear glass cut to the same size as the mat. It covered both the mat and the picture. The glass varied in grade from plate to common window glass and it was usually flat, although in the 1850's some convex glass was used. Occasionally, a casemaker would offer green-tinted glass in his line.

To bind the glass, mat, and photograph into a compact unit, a protector was quite often used. The exact date of its first use is not known; by 1850 it had become an almost necessary component. Its origin was probably due to an ingenious American adaptation of the original English picture holder of 1842 (see Fig. 10). The process of manufacturing a protector, sometimes called a "preserver," closely resembled that of making a mat. It was made from paper-thin malleable brass and was a frame of rectangular shape with an embossed border (one-sixteenth inch wide) on its inner margin edge. The embossed border created a picture frame effect to the viewing side of the photographic unit. The remaining part of the protector, when bent around the outer rim, locked the glass, mat, and photograph together. With the placing of the photographic unit between the velvet strip of the case bottom, the miniature case was completed (see Figs. 11 and 12).

Unfortunately, the leather miniature case manufacturers or assemblers rarely left their names imprinted on their products. It is to be assumed, as evidenced by the great variety of workmanship, designs, and accessories found, that hundreds of casemakers were in business when the leather case was at the peak of popularity. Furthermore, many of the makers were individual entrepreneurs who turned out only a limited supply, and business failures were undoubtedly commonplace due to poor management in the highly competitive trade. Scovill Manufacturing Co. and Edward T. Anthony Co., both volume producers of leather-covered cases owed their successful operation to their manufacture of many other items. Apparently only the handful of plastic case manufacturers protected by a patented process, were financially successful as miniature casemakers in the 1840-1860 era.

Possibly the first leather casemaker to mark his product with a name was Mathew B. Brady (see Fig. 13). His casemaking activities in New York City date from the early 1840's until around 1847 when he abandoned casemaking in favor of photography. From 1843 onward he was to become famous as one of the country's most talented daguerreotypists.

Another casemaker of the early and middle 1840's who imprinted his cases with his name was John Plumbe, Jr. Plumbe was a master organizer, promoter, as well as a man of vision. Back in 1836, Plumbe had dreamed of a cross-country railroad running from Maine to the Pacific Ocean. A surveyor by trade, he tried to convince Congress of the

Fig. 8. Popular mat styles for the miniature case. Top row, left to right: the elliptical, nonpareil, double elliptical. Lower row, left to right: the ornate elliptical, oval, octagon. In the 1840's the favored mat was the octagon; later in the 1850's, the ornate border became the rage.

Fig. 9. Hiram W. Hayden was issued a design patent for the above mat on Oct. 9, 1855. Other mat designs were later patented in the Civil War period.

Fig. 10. The English public favored a flip-top case rather than the book-style popular with Americans. The case shown measures 2½ x 3 inches (closed). On August 24, 1841, T. Wharton (Beard, Patentee) was issued an English patent for a mat and preserver. The patented pan-shaped metal preserver had a narrow holding edge to secure the glass, mat, and photograph into a unit (shown above without photograph). A rare case.

Fig. 11. The interior of a typical miniature case of the era. *Circa* 1844.

feasibility of his plan for a trans-continental railroad. By 1840 he was financially exhausted and in his own words, "was forced to take up the new art of daguerreotyping." In the next six years, Plumbe built a business empire through photography, opening one daguerreian parlor after another. Expanding to related fields, he began to manufacture the leather-covered miniature case about 1843 (*see* Fig. 14 and Plate 140). By 1846 he claimed to have at least 500 workers employed in his various enterprises. In trouble financially he sold his holdings to his employees in 1847. No record exists of what happened to his case manufacturing plant.

In the mid and latter part of the 1840's, several other names are identified with the manufacturing of the miniature case. The first of these was William Shew, listed in 1844 as a casemaker at 60½ Cornhill, Boston, Massachusetts. He with his brothers Myron, Jacob, and Trueman, were all con-nected with the photographic trades (*see* Fig. 15). Only Trueman, a daguerreian, did not make or distribute cases. William, in close association with Myron, continued making cases in Boston until 1850. In that year he left for San Fran-cisco, California, to resume his original trade as a daguerreian. Myron Shew advertised himself as a casemaker in Phila-delphia, Pennsylvania, both before and after 1850, as did Jacob Shew in Baltimore, Maryland (*see* Fig. 16). All of the leather cases of the Shew brothers show identical designs and workmanship.

Another Boston casemaker, "Studley and Gordon," oper-ated a "Miniature Case Manufactory" at 5 Hanover St. in 1846 and, like Shew, identified their case. Presumably the partnership was dissolved, for by 1848 Hiram Studley, using the single name Studley, was producing cases at a new Boston address. He was not listed as a casemaker after 1849.

In Philadelphia, in 1842, M. P. Simons in partnership with a Mr. Willis began making miniature cases at 173 Chestnut St. and continued until 1848 when Simons, like Brady and the Shew brothers, became a leading daguerreian. Willis continued to manufacture cases and in that year of 1848 formed a partnership with a Mr. Gordon, possibly the same Gordon of "Studley and Gordon." Neither Willis nor Simons imprinted their names in the cases they made.

Many small case factories were scattered throughout Connecticut in the 1840's. These producers of miniature cases did not stamp or mark with an identifying name, and even Scovill Manufacturing Company of Waterbury, Connecticut, perhaps the largest outlet of the era, while marking their daguerreotype plates clearly, did not identify the cases they sold.

In the first few years of the 1850's, despite the great num-

ber of leather-covered miniature cases made, only one maker is known to have had his name imprinted in the case. Levi Chapman of 102 William St., New York City, a leather and pocketbook merchant in the early 1840's, began making miniature cases sometime around 1847 (*see* Fig. 17). By 1850 he carried a full line not only of cases but other materials, for the photographic trade. He had two traveling agents on the road selling his wares in 1851 and 1852.

The case manufacturing situation began changing in the early 1850's. The mass-producer had slowly captured the market. New York City had become the center of the case supply trade. Largest of these suppliers was Edward T. Anthony Company, who by 1854 not only operated his own case factory but also made other parts and apparatus related to the photographic trade. He also offered a complete line of

Fig. 12. The daguerreian artist L. G. Chase of Boston, featured a top which was hinged open as a pair of tiny doors revealing the art within.

Fig. 13. Mathew B. Brady embossed his name (upper center) and his occupation, Casemaker, N. Y. (lower center) on the exterior front of his case.

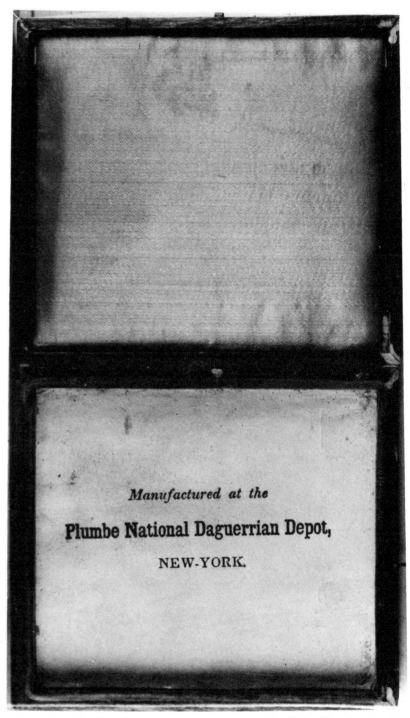

Manufactured at the

Plumbe National Daguerrian Depot,

NEW-YORK.

Fig. 14. The interior of a case manufactured by John Plumbe, Jr. C. 1843–45.

Figs. 15 & 16. The Shew Brothers, who manufactured cases and distributed them in Boston, Philadelphia, and Baltimore, were among the few miniature casemakers who placed advertising labels on the inside rear cover of their cases.

Fig. 17. An example of a casemaker identifying his product on the inside cover of a case. (Coll. of Jack T. Ericson).

raw materials to other casemakers ranging from leather skivers to silk and satin for cushions. Two other large casemakers having their main sales outlet in New York City were Scovill Manufacturing Company and Holmes, Booth and Hayden Company, both of Waterbury, Connecticut.

Throughout the decade of the fifties and well into the sixties there was a gradual cheapening of the wood-frame leather miniature case.[14] Embossed cloth, cardboard, cardboard and paper, were being substituted for the paper-thin leather. The demand for a better grade case was being met so well by the plastic "union" case that by 1870 the highly embossed leather case was a rarity. Only the traditional plain Morocco leather miniature case remained on the open market.

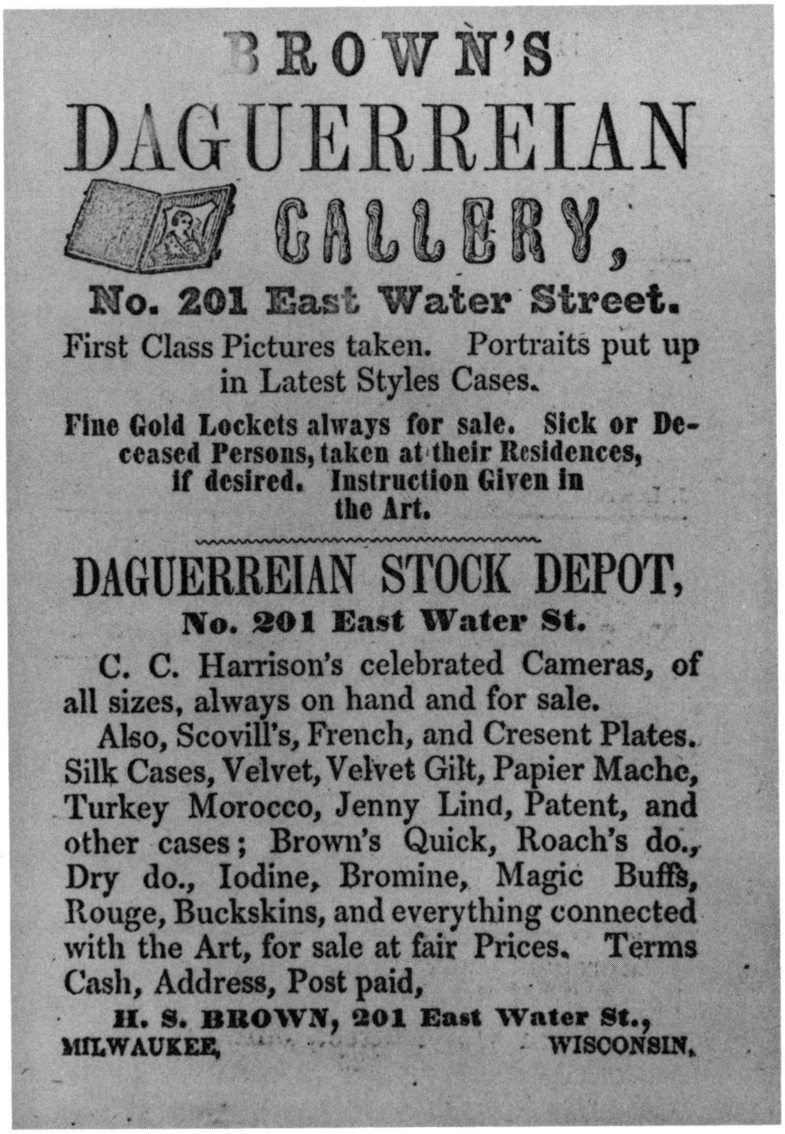

BROWN'S

DAGUERREIAN

GALLERY,

No. 201 East Water Street.

First Class Pictures taken.   Portraits put up in Latest Styles Cases.

Fine Gold Lockets always for sale. Sick or Deceased Persons, taken at their Residences, if desired. Instruction Given in the Art.

DAGUERREIAN STOCK DEPOT,

No. 201 East Water St.

C. C. Harrison's celebrated Cameras, of all sizes, always on hand and for sale.

Also, Scovill's, French, and Cresent Plates. Silk Cases, Velvet, Velvet Gilt, Papier Mache, Turkey Morocco, Jenny Lind, Patent, and other cases; Brown's Quick, Roach's do., Dry do., Iodine, Bromine, Magic Buffs, Rouge, Buckskins, and everything connected with the Art, for sale at fair Prices. Terms Cash, Address, Post paid,

H. S. BROWN, 201 East Water St.,
MILWAUKEE,   WISCONSIN,

Fig. 18. Case manufacturers often used wholesalers as an outlet for their products. Advertisement from Milwaukee, Wisconsin, City Directory, 1851.

2
The Thermoplastic Union Case

A different kind of miniature case was introduced to the public in the latter part of 1852. The new style cases were unique, they were the first plastic products to be patented and mass-produced in America. Like their leather counterparts, they were objects of art because the designs on their covers were made from dies originally cut by artist-engravers who were also diesinkers. The new plastic creations gained widespread popularity and were used well into the 1860's, and occasionally beyond, until the conventional photograph album became increasingly the rage, and the plastic cases began fading into obscurity.

The innovator of the plastic case was an imaginative and inventive Yankee named Samuel Peck of New Haven, Connecticut. Peck took up the art of daguerreotyping in 1844 as an associate with Tomlinson and Phineas Pardee, Jr. Photography was still in its infancy when Peck took over the New Haven photography studio in his own name in December, 1845. Benham's New Haven City Directory of 1846 carried an advertisement for the new establishment describing in glowing terms its decor and equipment. The advertisement reflected the typical Peck business acumen, proclaiming "All pictures made satisfactory or no sale. Persons that may feel disposed to favor with a sitting, will not be considered under any obligation to purchase a likeness, unless they choose after seeing them."

During his six years in photography, Peck was dissatisfied with the available daguerreotype plate holders, which were used to hold the thin silvered-copper plates so that they could be buffed to a mirror-like brilliancy before use in the camera. He devised an efficient, yet simple, plate holder and was issued a U. S. Patent (7,326) for it on April 30, 1850. His new and ingenious idea immediately caught the attention of Scovill Manufacturing Co., Waterbury, Connecticut, which lost no time in making contact with him. Although interested in Peck's new plate holder, its main interest in the enterprising Yankee was to form an association with him for the manufacturing of miniature cases to hold the pictures of the now booming photography industry. Obtaining good basic workmanship and attractively designed covers for miniature cases had become a prime concern and an increasing problem to the Scovill firm in its efforts to meet the multiplying demand of photographers throughout the East. Scovill's business-like approach must have persuaded Peck to accept their proposition; he left his studio by December, 1850, in preparation for a closer relationship with the Scovill Company. A factory site was selected in New Haven, and the newly formed firm took on the name "Samuel Peck and Co." An informal partnership took effect, but it was not formalized until March, 1851.[1]

At first Peck made his cases along traditional lines, following the methods used throughout the 1840's. He soon decided, however, to add a new line of papier-mâché miniature cases. It must have occurred to Peck that if he could use a composition adaptable for molding a deeper and more striking design, he could develop a case which might surpass the prettily stamped or die-embossed leather or paper-covered cases then in vogue. Whether Peck's idea for experimenting with plastic

Fig. 19. The case shown has a molded plastic piece applied directly to the wood frame in place of the conventional leather "top." It is not known whether this was a transitional case or one made to compete with those of plastic composition. (Coll. of J. Harry Du Bois)

Fig. 20. The above press mold was used in the S. Peck and Co. factory at New Haven, Connecticut. It is presently displayed at the Mattatuck Historical Society, Waterbury, Connecticut. (Coll. of J. Harry Du Bois)

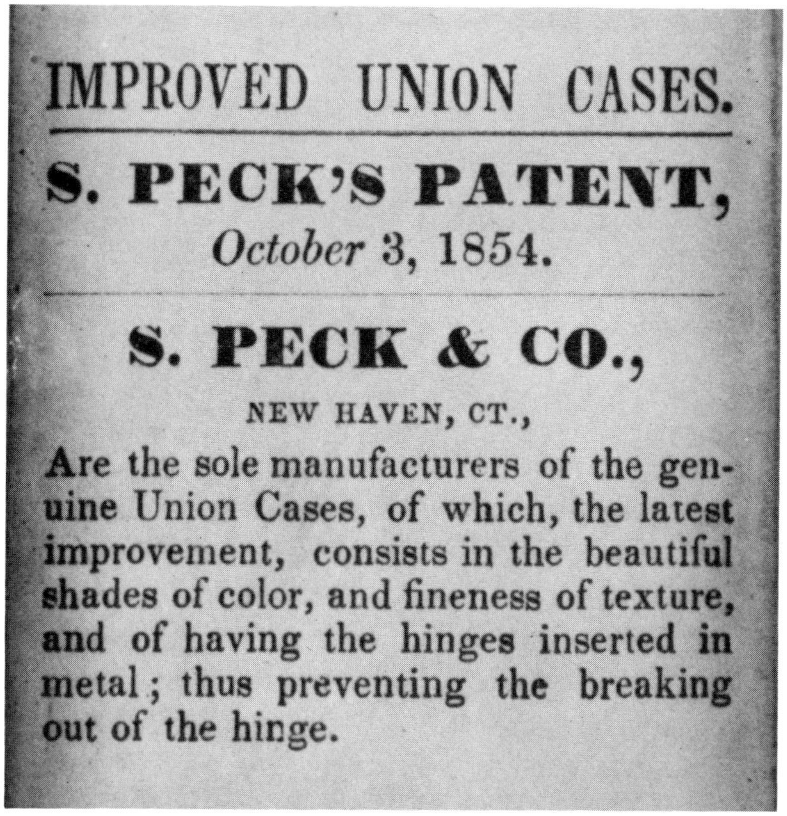
IMPROVED UNION CASES.

S. PECK'S PATENT,
October 3, 1854.

S. PECK & CO.,
NEW HAVEN, CT.,

Are the sole manufacturers of the genuine Union Cases, of which, the latest improvement, consists in the beautiful shades of color, and fineness of texture, and of having the hinges inserted in metal; thus preventing the breaking out of the hinge.

Fig. 21. Samuel Peck's label for identifying his 1854 patent plastic daguerreotype case.

Fig. 22. A case label showing the merging of the Peck and Halvorson patents.

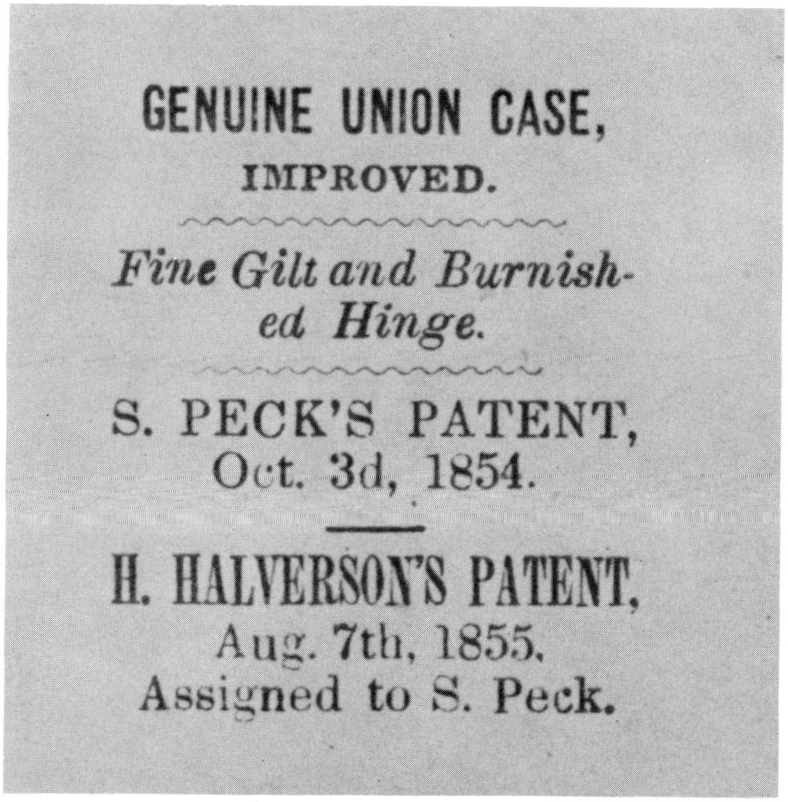
GENUINE UNION CASE,
IMPROVED.

Fine Gilt and Burnished Hinge.

S. PECK'S PATENT,
Oct. 3d, 1854.

H. HALVERSON'S PATENT,
Aug. 7th, 1855,
Assigned to S. Peck.

composition stemmed from his work with papier-mâché, or whether he invented the composition is not known, but he did begin his experiments in May, 1852. He succeeded during the next few months in working out the right combination of die molds, plastic composition, and heating methods for his process of making a new style daguerreotype case.[2] As with most inventors, Peck ran into difficulty at times when his heated rollers for pressing the composition failed and his ovens proved inadequate to withstand the high heats required for his process. Dies were a problem, too, because they were larger than those used for ordinary button designs.

Although Peck's cases were perfected and on the market by early 1853, he was not issued a U. S. Patent until October 3, 1854 (11,758) (*see* Fig. 21). In his patent application he described the materials he used as "composed of gum shellac and woody fibers or other suitable fibrous material dyed to the color that may be required and ground with the shellac and between hot rollers so as to be converted into a mass which when heated becomes plastic so that it can be pressed into a mold or between dies and made to take the form that may be imparted to it by such dies."[3] Peck went on to explain the use of thick paper or thin pasteboard so that "when the dies are forced together so as to form the half of a case or box, the said paper or pasteboard shall be made to adhere to and line the entire surface against which it is pressed by the die." If the paper was gilded and burnished before the application, the whole impression of the mold, or the part where the paper was placed, gave the finished product a burnished gilded appearance much the same as produced by applying gold leaf —a far more laborious process. Peck's process entailed gilding sheets of paper, holding the burnished side directly against the surface of the die and then compressing the paper upon the plastic compound. The result was a beautiful, polished gilt impression which when combined with the composition gave it great strength and resistance to breakage or cracking.[4] His process also rendered the case non-porous, thereby protecting it from atmospheric conditions.

A few weeks after his patent was issued, Samuel Peck received a letter dated December 16, 1854, from the patent office: "Upon reading and filing the affidavit of Halvor Halvorson made the 13th inst., it is hereby ordered that the day of hearing of the interference between your patent for improvements in making daguerreotype cases and the application of Horace Barnes, assignee of H. Halvorson for the alleged improvements, be extended to the 1st Monday of February next and the said Barnes has been notified thereof." Another letter from the patent office followed, dated February 7, 1855, which again postponed the date until August 1855— "as requested by joint application of the parties. . . ."[5] Halvor-

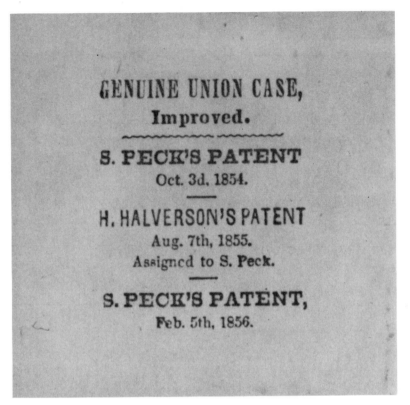

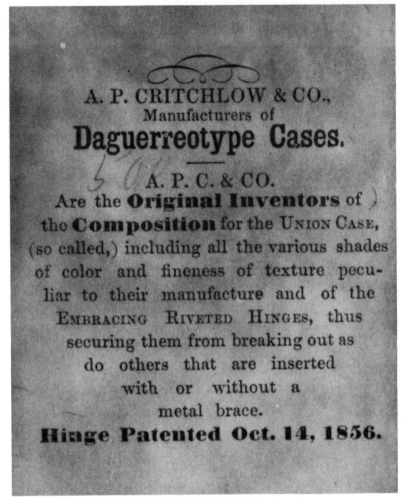

Fig. 23. The case label encompasses the three patents used by Samuel Peck.

Fig. 24. Critchlow, like Peck, identified his product with a label inside the case under the photographic unit.

son's patent was granted August 7, 1855 (13,410). According to labels on the rear of some "Union" cases, the patents were merged (*see* Fig. 22).

Although Samuel Peck was the first man to patent and mass produce the daguerreotype case as a pioneer plastic product, a natural plastic substance had already been in use for some years. In 1843 a surgeon named Dr. William Montgomerie informed the Royal Society of Arts in London, that in Malaya he had seen knife handles and other articles made from a vegetable plastic material obtained from the gutta percha tree which grew in a very limited region near the equator. The gummy substance was softened in hot water, molded by hand to the desired shape and then hardened and cooled. When the potential of this natural substance became known abroad, it was used for a multitude of purposes. The photography industry for instance found that utensils made of this acid-resistant material were excellent for holding chemicals. The rubber-like gutta percha, because of its electrical insulating properties, was widely adopted as an insulating covering for cable and telegraph wires. Although the plastic daguerreotype case was later frequently referred to as "gutta percha" or "hard rubber," no evidence exists that this natural material was actually used in the molding of Union cases; but we do know that gutta percha was used to form some decorative objects in other fields.

The tremendous demand for gutta percha in Europe and America from the mid-1840's onward must have fostered a considerable search for a suitable substitute. Besides Samuel Peck another known experimenter in developing a plastic compound adaptable for the molding of daguerreotype cases was Alfred P. Critchlow. A diesinker and horn button-maker from Birmingham, England, Critchlow came to America and settled in Haydenville, Massachusetts in 1843. In the mid-

SPRAY OF FLOWERS, VARIANT

Casemaker: Unknown
Papier-mâché, 3⅛″ X 2⅝″, C. 1855
Inlaid mother-of-pearl

THE RED RECTANGLE

Casemaker: Unknown
Velvet on cardboard & wood frame,
3¾″ X 3½″, C. 1854

A TINY GOLDEN ROSE

Casemaker: Unknown
Leather, 3⅝″ X 3⅛″, C. 1848

LOUIS M. DAGUERRE

Casemaker: Unknown
Leather, 3⅝″ X 3⅛″, C. 1848

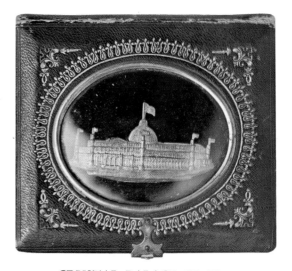

CRYSTAL PALACE, N. Y.

Casemaker: Unknown
Leather, glass enclosed design, 3⅜″ X 3⅞″, C. 1854

Coll. of Mrs. Lucille Boss

SPRAY OF FLOWERS

Casemaker: Unknown
Papier-mâché, 3⅞" X 3⅜", C. 1854
Inlaid mother-of-pearl

TULIPS AND ROSES

Casemaker: Unknown
Celluloid on wood frame, 3¾" X 3¼", C. 1870
Inlaid mother-of-pearl

Coll. of J. Harry Du Bois

THE GREEN RECTANGLE

Casemaker: Unknown
Velvet on cardboard & wood frame,
3¾" X 3⅜", C. 1853

THE OPEN MINIATURE CASE

Casemaker: Unknown
Leather, 4¾" X 3¾" (closed) C. 1851

Courtesy of Time-Out Antiques, N.Y.

Two velvet-covered cases for twins.
The linings are of satin. Both are
one-sixteenth size.

forties he moved to a new location in Florence, Massachusetts, where he continued his occupation of making buttons. Over the years Critchlow gradually developed machinery, dies and a plastic compound for producing the new style cases; he began manufacturing them in 1853 by working his establishment in two twelve-hour shifts.[6] His black plastic composition was believed to have been made from a combination of shellac, wood resin, and lampblack; it was known as the "Florence Compound" and was mixed on mill roll type equipment.[7]

Eventually, both Peck and Critchlow, working independently, began experimenting with hinge improvements. The first to succeed was Samuel Peck. He was issued on February 5, 1856, a U.S. Patent (14,202) for "Fastening for the Hinges of Daguerreotype Cases" (see Fig. 23). In his patent application Peck noted that in daguerreotype cases of plastic material, "the hinges have been fastened by rivets through the material or by some adhesive gum. The material of the case when cold is very brittle and nearly thirty percent of the cases were spoiled by breaking them in riveting on the hinges; and when the cases were put in use a slight twist or fall was liable to break off the hinge where it was fastened, thus spoiling the case." Peck's improved hinge was a metal reinforcement encased in molded plastic.[8] He states in his patent: "The combination of metal straps or supports with the material of the case when the same is plastic so as to strengthen the case and form a secure fastening for the hinges . . ."

Peck's 1856 patent led the way for two other hinge patents for plastic daguerreotype cases. Alfred P. Critchlow was issued a hinge patent on October 14, 1856 (15,915) (see Fig. 24). His hinges can often be recognized by their embracing "rosette" type rivets which often appear to the eye as part of the total design (also later used by Littlefield, Parsons & Co.) (see Fig. 25).

A later hinge patent was issued on June 1, 1858 (20,436) to Edward G. Kinsley and Samuel A. W. Parker Jr., both of Stoughton, Massachusetts, for "Hinge for Daguerreotype and Other Cases." Their patent claimed that "the strain on the hinge during the act of opening or shutting the box will be completely removed from the said sides in a direction at right angles to their inner surface." The inventors further claimed an "improved mode of arraying and applying hinge with reference to the side and end or the end and bottom of either half of the box, that is extending the hinge leaf through the side of the half and against the inner surface of its end or the same and the inner surface of the bottom and fastening such leaf to the end or to the end and bottom." Their innovation was a friction throw-type hinge (see Fig. 26). Plastic cases were produced under their patent by Wadham's Manufacturing Co.

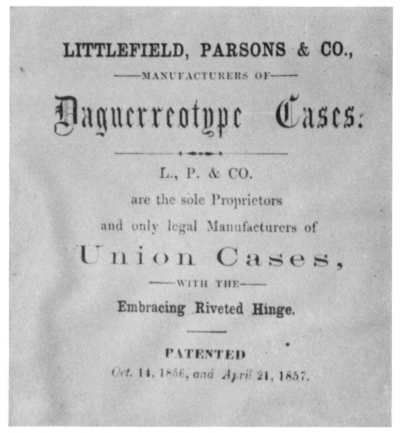

Fig. 25. A. P. Critchlow sold his Union Case Manufacturing Co. to Littlefield, Parsons & Co. in 1857.

The next important patent issued for the plastic Union case was for the improvement of the plastic composition itself. A U.S. Patent was issued August 24, 1858 (21,285) for "An Improvement in Composition for Daguerreotype Cases, Buttons and Other Uses." The inventor was Mark Tomlinson of Birmingham, Connecticut. He describes his composition "as equal parts, by weight, of shellac, Breckenridge or cannel-coal, and ivory black. The shellac and cannel-coal are first finely pulverized separately, and the three ingredients are then well mixed together and fed between a pair of steam heated rollers, one of which rotates at a higher velocity than the other, and are thereby ground into a pasty mass, which while still hot and plastic is cut or divided by a spatula or other instrument into cakes of sufficient size to form the articles or pieces to be made. These pieces are laid upon a metal plate or tray and placed in an oven heated by steam or other agency and allowed to remain therein for about 10 or 15 minutes, after which taken out and while still hot are placed in steam heated dies of the requisite form to produce

Fig. 26. A Wadham's plastic case measuring 3¾₁₆″ x 2¹¹₁₆″, illustrating the friction throw-type hinge manufactured under the Kinsley & Parker patent. (Coll. of Mrs. Janie Wright)

the articles or forms desired, and therein subjected to a heavy pressure. The pieces or articles are then allowed to cool in the dies to a degree sufficient to enable them to be taken out without any danger of bending or otherwise injuring their form." In heating his rollers, oven and dies, he used steam at a pressure of about 80 pounds to the square inch, he adds. Articles made of this composition he said would "neither warp nor have their surface spotted or injured in appearance by water, like the composition of shellac and sawdust, which is used for similar articles, and his composition possesses a greater degree of tenacity or less degree of liability to fracture."[9]

In 1857 two of the leading figures in the manufacture of the Union daguerreotype cases left their respective established

businesses. In 1855 the "co-partnership" between the Scovill Manufacturing Co. and Samuel Peck had been formalized by the chartering of a joint stock company under the title "Samuel Peck and Company."[10] But a growing rift of indeterminate cause between the Scovill Company and Peck made them part company in 1857.[11] Peck's interests were purchased by the Scovill Company for $20,000, and he was given an additional amount of $7,500, possibly for vacating the plant.[12] Management of the New Haven factory then came under the jurisdiction of the New York store. Alfred P. Critchlow, who in 1853 had as partners Samuel L. Hill and Isaac Parsons, sold his business sometime in 1857, and the new firm became known as Littlefield, Parsons and Co. The business

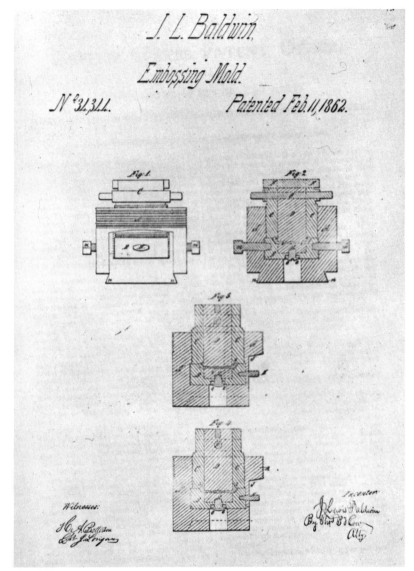

Fig. 27. An improvement for the molding of plastic cases was invented by J. Lewis Baldwin of Newark, New Jersey. The patent drawing is shown.

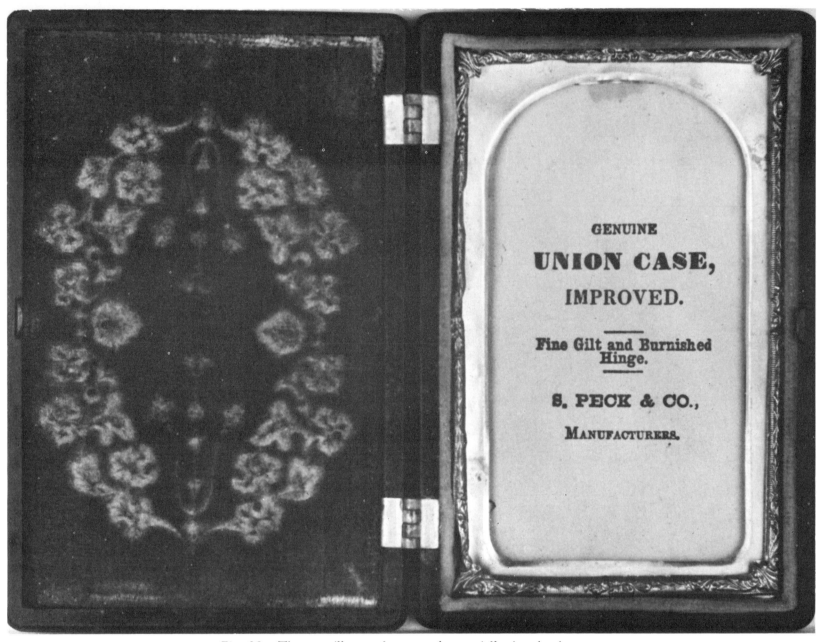

Fig. 28. The case illustrated was made especially for the ferrotype (tintype) and measured 2½″ x 3¾″. It was made by Scovill Manufacturing Co. probably after Peck had left the New Haven plant in 1857. Competitive paper-covered wood frame cases for the ferrotype were also available in this era.

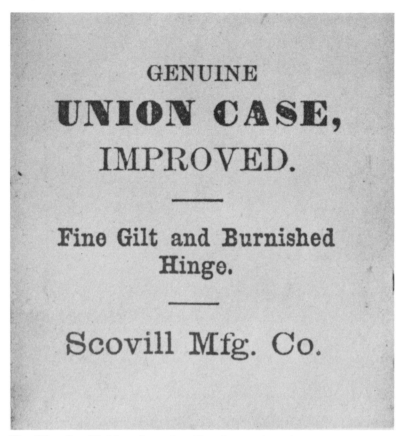

GENUINE
UNION CASE,
IMPROVED.

Fine Gilt and Burnished Hinge.

Scovill Mfg. Co.

Fig. 29. Scovill Manufacturing Co. also marked the plastic case with their own label.

continued its operation under this name until a corporation called Florence Manufacturing Company was formed on May 23, 1866 (*see* Fig. 31). The new company was organized by George A. Burr, Isaac S. Parsons and David G. Littlefield. After it was in operation a short while it became evident that the steadily decreasing demand for daguerreotype cases made it impossible to rely on their manufacture for a main source of income. Photography had turned to paper photographs and tintypes almost exclusively. A change in policy resulted and other products such as buttons, jewel and revolver boxes and later, brushes were gradually substituted in place of the plastic picture cases. The few remaining case manufacturers were turning to other fields and products.

In retrospect as the plastic case era came to a close, the composition of the finely ground ingredients of the early days of Peck and Critchlow, had not only created a thing of artistic beauty—a molded miniature case—but had also pioneered an entirely new field of industry—plastics.

Fig. 30. The case shown here exemplifies a typical plastic case made during the early 1860's. (Coll. of J. Harry Du Bois)

Fig. 31. This illustrates an inside label from The Florence Manufacturing Co. Littlefield, Parsons & Co. adopted this new name on May 23, 1866. (Coll. of Mrs. Janie Wright)

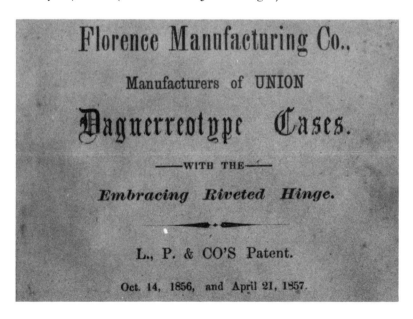

Florence Manufacturing Co.,

Manufacturers of UNION

Daguerreotype Cases.

---WITH THE---

Embracing Riveted Hinge.

L., P. & CO'S Patent.

Oct. 14, 1856, and April 21, 1857.

3
Novelty Items and Other Cases

As early as 1840, women wore lockets containing tiny photographic images about the size of a dime, in the old tradition of miniature paintings. This custom continued from the 1840's well into the 1860's. Very small daguerreotypes were also set into rings, breast-brooches, pins, bracelets, and even in the heads of canes. In 1846, Samuel Peck advertised that he could furnish daguerreotypes in "finger rings, round gold Hunting lockets, oval gold lockets, open fine gold lockets, open plate lockets, open double gilt lockets, satin cases, silk velvet, and in Mahogany, Black Walnut, and Rosewood frames." The favorite containers, however, for daguerreotypes and other types of photographs until about 1870 were the rectangular paper-thin leather, paper, or cloth-covered miniature cases. Variations of these picture cases began to appear about 1850, and even before in some instances. Some of the new models were unusual, some ornate, and others handsomely plain.

The first unusual daguerreotype case was patented by a woman—Ann F. Stiles of Southbury, Connecticut (*see* Fig. 34). A United States Letters Patent for her invention was issued January 22, 1850 (7,041). Her design included a glass tube or case in which a picture could be conveniently secured and seen through a special lens which magnified the image at the same time that it offered protection from dust and reflections from outside objects. The Stiles' case was conical; the diameter across the bottom was 2¾ inches, and it tapered

upward so that the width across the top was 1½ inches. Its height was 3 inches. The magnified viewer was designed to let in light, but the inside was darkened with paint to cut the glare from the daguerreotype's mirrored surface. The Stiles' Magnifying Case, as it was named, was manufactured solely by Japhet Curtis of Southford, Connecticut.[1] It was stocked by several dealers of daguerreotype materials; and it was advertised and carried by the Scovill Manufacturing Co.

The Stiles' Magnifying Case was the forerunner of a folding stereoscopic daguerreotype case invented by John F. Mascher of Philadelphia. Mascher was one of those tinkering Americans of the era, who had patented a fan and flywheel regulator in 1849 to be used on clocks and music boxes. Inspired by an article in the *Scientific American* describing the workings of an English stereoscope which used two almost identical daguerreotypes, Mascher constructed an improved version of the English viewing device. He described his stereoscopic viewer in an enthusiastic letter to the editors of the *Scientific American,* published on June 26, 1852. On March 8, 1853, Mascher was issued a U.S. patent (9,611) for a folding stereoscopic daguerreotype case which incorporated some of the features of his earlier stereoscope viewer box. The case's interior had a simple arrangement—a supplementary lid or flap in which were fitted two ordinary magnifying lenses. The two daguerreotype pictures which he placed in the case had been photographed at an angle of about 25 degrees

WILLARD & CO'S
Daguerreotype,
PHOTOGRAPHIC
AND
Ambrotype Goods,
Of every description.

Fig. 32. A label found in the rear of a plastic case bore this typical jobber's advertisement. The case was manufactured by Holmes, Booth and Hayden, a maker of plastic cases in the later 1850's and the 60's. (Coll. of Mrs. Janie Wright)

Fig. 33. The black plastic locket, 1¼ inches by 1½ inches, shown here, was fashioned for two pictures. The butterfly decorations were metal—one of gold, the other silver. (Coll. of Mrs. Lucille Boss)

PATENT CASE.

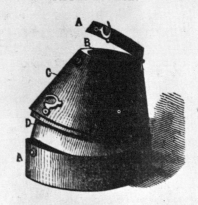

The above cut represents a new style of case called by the inventress, "Magnifying Daguerreotype Case," invented and patented by Miss ANN F. STILES, Southbury, Conn., Mr. Japhet Curtis, Jr. Southbury, Conn., is the sole manufacturer.

This case presents a circular form, its diameter across the bottom is 2 3-4 inches, do. across the top 1 1-2 inches, and when closed it is 3 inches high. A A. are covers which are attached to the body by silver plated hinges. Each cover when closed is made fast by a hook. C. the body covered, like the covers, with fine morocco leather, and represents a tube, or hollow cone. In the top of this tube, B. is a plano-convex lens, which is so arranged, that the principle focus falls upon the impression when it is inclosed in the ground glass tube D. The Daguerreotype plate is cut to fit the tube D., in which there is a groove to secure the plate and mat, which is sealed by the common sticking paper. This is a very curious and ingenious contrivance to display the Daguerreotype Portrait. It magnifies the impression several times larger than it appears to the naked eye, and when accompanied with a fine, clear toned, and highly finished impression it adds life and beauty to its appearance.

Fig. 34. Stiles' Magnifying Case.

39

and "one-half." The "sixth" size model was supplied in embossed leather with two hooks, "imitation Turkey Morocco leather snap case," or Union case.

The declining popularity of Mascher's case was probably due to the fact that the daguerreotype was not adaptable because of its reflective qualities and to the high cost of the case's manufacture. Mascher attempted to improve the versatility of his case in 1856, but larger box-type stereo-viewers were already being produced in this period.[3] These offered greater flexibility in that the pictures of glass or paper could be changed at will.

In 1855 Mascher secured another U. S. patent (12,257) for a similar device in the form of a stereoscopic medallion, which resembled an ordinary locket when closed. Two sup-

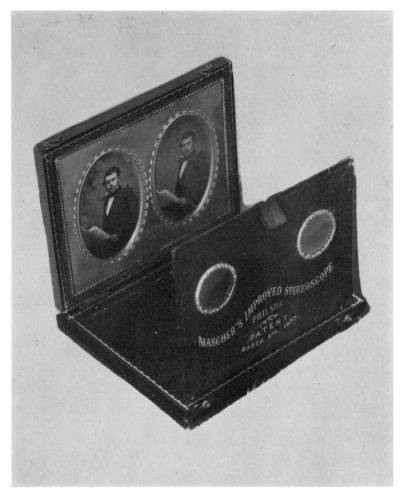

Fig. 35. An early stereoscope. When viewed through the twin magnifying glasses, the two likenesses of the unknown musician blend into a single three-dimensional portrait.

or 30 degrees on the right and left line between the camera and the subject (*see* Fig. 35).[2]

The idea of stereoscopic viewing had caught on in America following the Crystal Palace Exhibition of 1851 in London, where the Brewster Stereoscope made its public debut. However, little had been done with the stereoscope in America until Mascher devised his improvement on the English model. Some of America's leading photographers who had been experimenting with stereoscopic daguerreotypes viewed Mascher's patent case with interest. His small and compact case offered photography studio patrons a fascinating three-dimensional view of themselves. Its popularity was short-lived but intense. Edward Anthony, New York City, daguerreotype supply jobber and manufacturer, carried Mascher's cases in stock in three different sizes, "one-sixth," "one-quarter,"

Fig. 36. An imitation tortoise shell miniature case measuring $3\frac{1}{8}$ inches by $2\frac{5}{8}$ inches. The book-style case has a colorful hand-painted decoration. Manufacturer unknown.

peared in the 1840's, but did not become really popular until around 1850 (*see* Fig. 37). Many of these new book-style models were made of papier-mâché, a material well suited for miniature cases because of its strength and board-like quality. It also provided a perfect base for decorative inlay work, using mother-of-pearl, or for other artistic ornamentation.

Papier-mâché for the picture case was made by pasting or glueing together sheets of paper which were then submitted to powerful pressure to lend greater durability. The addition of sulphate of iron, quicklime, glue, or white of eggs to the pulp rendered it partially waterproof; the addition of borax and phosphate of soda made the finished product fireproof.[5]

Mother-of-pearl designs were laid on a soft ground of black varnish (japan) with which the papier-mâché board had been coated. A variety of mother-of-pearl known as "Aurora" was widely used for decorative inlay because of its brilliant colors; white pearl was also popular for inlay. The shell ma-

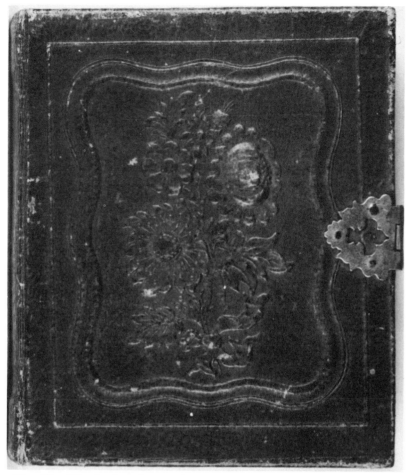

Fig. 37. The book-style case shown above was manufactured by Levi Chapman of New York City about 1849. (Coll. of Jack T. Ericson)

plementary lids each contained a lens, which folded up inside the medallion lid and stood opposite when opened, converting the medallion into a stereoscope. The cost for Mascher's medallion was twelve dollars.[4]

Mascher pursued his interest in daguerreotype cases, in general; on February 10, 1857 he secured a U. S. patent (16,600) for a process of ornamenting daguerreotype cases. His idea called for covering the cases with stained or colored paper in imitation of tortoise-shell, wood-grains, marble, etc. The covers were then coated with a combination of gelatin (fine transparent glue) and bichromate of potash which water-proofed and preserved the surface (*see* Fig. 36). In his patent he suggested the same kind of paper used by book-binders or house decorators which "could be obtained in great variety."

Daguerreotype cases made in the form of books first ap-

Fig. 38. A typical mother-of-pearl miniature case inlaid on papier-mâché.

terial was sliced into thin layers by a process patented in 1833 and was usually cut with scissors and knives, although some regular forms were stamped by a press.[6] After the design was formed, the board was hardened in an oven, then varnished again; it was next rubbed down with pumice stone and water, re-varnished and placed in the oven to harden again (correct temperature, about 280 degrees Fahrenheit, was important for a glassy finish). The process was repeated until the coats of varnish made the entire surface of the papier-mâché board level with the design. Any ornamental lines, gold leaf, or writing were then applied by hand. The edges of the "book" were gilt-painted to simulate pages and the hinge was

Fig. 40. Two identical velvet-covered oval cases—one in blue, the other in red. The linings are satin. Both are of "one-sixteenth" size.

Fig. 39. Successor to the colorful papier-mâché case was one of wood frame covered with celluloid. The above example is inlaid with mother-of-pearl and measures 3⅞ inches by 3⅜ inches. An American inventor, John Wesley Hyatt, produced and patented in July, 1870, a durable and colorful thermoplastic—celluloid, which was a combination of cellulose nitrate and camphor. The composition became the first good semi-synthetic plastic. (Coll. of J. Harry Du Bois)

usually inscribed in gold with such appropriate words as "token," "souvenir," or 'bijou' (little jewel). Closures were either clasp-hinges or snap-style fastenings.

Another technique used for mother-of-pearl designs entailed placing pieces of white pearl on the soft ground of japan varnish. Forms of flowers or other designs were laid on in various thicknesses, the thickest parts forming the highlights; damp powdered colors were then applied for effect, and the whole was finished with colors mixed with varnish.[7] The papier-mâché board was then made waterproof and finished by the method described earlier (*see* Fig. 38).

Other variations of inlay work used hand-painted landscape

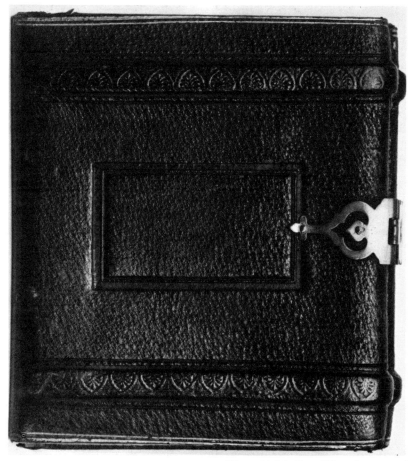 

Figs. 41 & 42. The photo on the left pictures the original Eichmeyer leather-covered case patented Feb. 27, 1855. At right is a quality imitation in pigskin.

scenes bordered by mother-of-pearl. Some inlay designs on book-type cases were centered with cameo or carved tops. Inlaid mother-of-pearl was also used on tortoise shell cases.

Inlay work was laborious because of the generally small size of the shell pieces, and the intricate task of arranging light and shade artistically. The idea for using inlaid pearl work on miniature cases probably stemmed from decorated snuff boxes—an eighteenth century art craft plied by jewelers and enamelers. The snuff boxes often used mother-of-pearl inlay and natural silver on tortoise shell. America's interest in the Far East during the 1850's was reflected in Oriental-type book-style cases with mother-of-pearl designs that were embellished with gold, red, or other bright paint against a glassy jet-black background.[8]

Other variations of the book-style case had morocco leather coverings, or used velvet in varied hues; they usually had hinge-clasp closures. One handsome black leather case had a tooled gold cover with a leaf scroll design which contrasted effectively against the nubby surface of the morocco leather. Another smaller model of a "one-sixteenth" size had a velvet top and "Turkey morocco" sides and bottom with snap closure.

A square velvet-covered book-case, lined in watered silk, in the popular "sixth" size was named after Jenny Lind, the famous Swedish opera star, who took the country by storm during her American singing tour in 1850. Such cases often had cameo inserts in the front center of the cover and were available in various colors.[9] Fasteners were clasp-type hinges or snap closures. Also available in the 1850's were oval velvet-covered cases, brass-hinged and lined with watered silk; these were often fitted with convex French crystal glass and snapped closed (*see* Fig. 40).

A new model joined the clasp-hinged cases in the mid-fifties; it was a variation of the popular rectangular miniature case.

A design patent (694) was issued to Henry A. Eichmeyer of Philadelphia, on February 27, 1855, for a case design which would later be referred to as "band". A handsomely styled and leather-covered case, its design was unusual in that the two edges on which the hinges and clasps were respectively placed were rounded. The effect of the two parallel lines placed proportionally apart in relief gave an appearance of a case encircled by bands (see Fig. 41). In the late 1850's and into the 1860's, cheaper copies of this style were made of cardboard and covered with paper; the distinctive rounded edges were missing, although the hinge-clasp treatment was the same.

Another variation on the leather-covered case appeared in 1856. A U. S. patent (14,501) was issued to Halvor Halvorson of Boston, Massachusetts, on March 25, 1856; the assignor of the patent was Slocum and Watkinson. Halvorson intended his design as an "improvement in miniature cases," noting in his patent application that miniature cases should be made of stiff material to prevent possible injury to the picture enclosed within. His improvement consisted of a metal back and a metal surrounding frame. Inside, he proposed to substitute velvet covered glass for the conventional brass mat. The outer edges of the leather-covered case were hinged together (see Fig. 42).

The late 1850's saw the beginning of an American fad for photographs of calling-card size. First introduced in Paris by Desdéri, the court photographer of Napoleon III, the fashionable card photograph, named *carte de visite,* spread to London and the United States, and by 1860 had won general acceptance throughout America. The paper photographs, measuring about 2½ inches by 4 inches after mounting, were seldom larger than 2⅛ inches by 3½ inches unframed. Their size, ease of handling, and low cost made them suitable for mailing to distant friends or relatives. With the advent of cheaper photography, an innumerable amount of pictures were taken; the traditional album was introduced as a practical holder for the growing number of family portraits.[10]

Charles D. Fredericks, a New York photographer and photographic supply dealer, who was one of the pioneers in introducing the *carte de visite* to America, advertised in the *American Journal of Photography,* 1860: "Albums for 200, 100, 50, 30, 20 pictures. A new and beautiful article for the *carte de visite*" (see Fig. 46).

Albums ran the same gamut in cover designs as the miniature case—from highly ornate to starkly simple. They were usually leather-covered and had large elaborate brass hinge-type clasps, reminiscent of the book-style miniature cases. Prices ranged from a few cents for the inexpensive paper-covered models to about forty dollars for the finest quality

Fig. 43. A steel frame leather-covered miniature case made expressly for the ambrotype. When opened, the moveable center section, as shown above, contained the transparent glass photograph which when pressed against either velvet lining presented a clear picture.

Fig. 44. An all steel leather-covered case was patented by Halvor Halvorson on March 25, 1856.

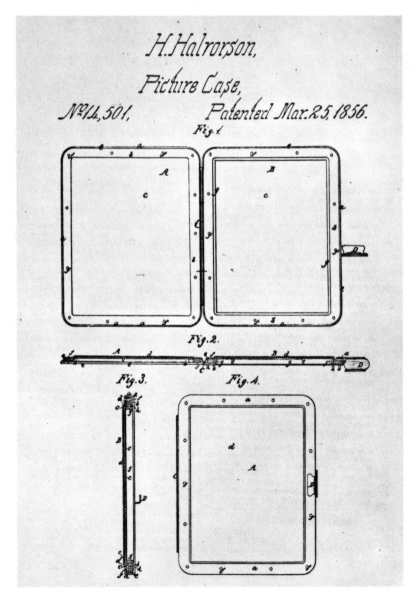

Fig. 45. A novelty "look-in" plastic case measuring $2\frac{11}{16}$ inches by $2\frac{1}{4}$ inches. An oval was molded in the case cover and clear glass placed inside. Other than this unique feature, the case was conventional in every respect. The article was manufactured by S. Peck and Co. under the Peck and Halvorson patents. Die design by F. Key. (Coll. of Mrs. Janie Wright)

Fig. 47. The above illustrates a plastic frame measuring $4\frac{3}{4}$ inches by $4\frac{1}{4}$ inches. It was molded to hold a standard photographic unit. The same unit was interchangeable for use in the miniature case. (Coll. of Emerick Hanzl, Jr.)

Fig. 46. An early leather-covered album tooled in gold. It was manufactured to hold paper photographs of calling-card size (*carte de visite*). The above measures 5 inches by $6\frac{1}{4}$ inches and bears the original date, Feb., 1864.

45

leather ones.[11] After 1860, miniature cases began increasingly to lose their former quality of craftsmanship and beauty. Many were now made of paper-covered wood, cardboard, or covered with waterproof cloth. The cheapening process was possibly due to competition with the album and the plastic case as well as Civil War conditions.

The infinite variety of designs and skills involved in the producing the vast array of picture containers was astounding. By 1850 the patron of the photographic gallery had a choice of framing his portrait in anything from cases costing merely pennies to expensive models of the finest quality and craftsmanship. Women could select a locket of any desired size and styling. Those who wished to hang their portraits on the wall could choose handsome frames made of choice woods, composition plastic (after 1853), or gilt-painted papier-mâché (see Fig. 47). From 1860 onward, the photographic album supplied the entire family's need for a picture container.

America's miniature case industry and the related manufacture of picture frames reached their full flower with the development of photography. Miniature case art reached the masses by the 1850's and, because of its wide variety of interesting designs became one of the most intriguing art crafts to come out of the nineteenth century.

4

Designs in Relief

Americans had become increasingly familiar with art in the era before the Civil War. Exhibitions, art unions, art institutes, and fairs displayed, in the various cities and towns, a variety of arts and crafts for public viewing. They fostered an aesthetic awareness among the people and stimulated a continuing development of artistic expression.

The miniature case industry, as did so many of its American craft counterparts, sought to create a desire and demand for its product by offering a variety of design themes, which would appeal to the taste and pocketbook of a widely divergent public. American taste of the period see-sawed from utter simplicity to a high level of sophistication; but whatever the taste, good or bad, the embossed designs on the covers of the miniature case reflected the preferences of the American public.

The designs embossed in leather, as well as those of the popular and less expensive paper and cloth covers, were usually produced by brass die cylinders. These were especially fashioned with raised figures made for embossing paper-thin materials. The cylinder-dies were then used in a heavy screw-type press for the embossing process.[1]

The original dies were prepared by die-engravers as a work of art. The men employed in this trade were variously known as engravers, diesinkers, letter cutters, or seal engravers. It was their task to create a thing of beauty, an achievement which would define the art of the miniature case. Unfortunately, few diemakers left their signatures on leather, cloth, or paper-covered designs. Possibly the earliest artist to emboss

his name on a daguerreotype case cover design was B. C. True of Albany, New York (*see* Fig. 6). Also in the mid-1840's, the name Pretlove (David Pretlove) appears on several well designed floral motifs (*see* Plates 116, 123, 130, 133). In the 1850 decade A. C. Paquet and C. Loekle, both of Philadelphia, were among the few designers who identified their art on case covers. Paquet created an elaborate flower motif which was embossed on silk (*see* Plate 146). Loekle designed a bouquet of flowers tied with a ribbon inscribed "Forget Me Not" (*see* Plate 174).

Environmental influences of the era played a significant part in the types of designs selected to ornament the miniature case during its period of peak popularity. Much early case design reflected Greek and Roman inspiration. The influence of Greek style architecture in America from the early 1800's combined with a native feeling toward Greek traditions and literature, was reflected in many patterns found on case covers. The lyre, long a historic ornament and often represented in Greek art in scenes of domestic life and mythological settings, was frequently seen in various forms on daguerreotype cases. An early example of the lyre motif was made by casemaker Mathew B. Brady, circa 1843 (*see* Fig. 13). More elaborate designs using the lyre motif were also used in leather, paper-covered, or plastic cases in the 1850's.

The simplicity and grace of Greek decorative art, its balanced and symmetrical composition, are reflected in the many Grecian urns or vases depicted on the covers of miniature cases. An early and particularly outstanding example of this

47

influence is evidenced on a leather-covered case, "The Grecian Urn," circa 1843 (*see* Plate 140). Also used by the case industry were numerous geometric forms—the circle with tangents, the diamond, all representing "the Geometric age"—a historic Greek design period.

America's tremendous interest in nature strongly influenced design during the 1840-1850 period. This love of nature was evident in the arts of the period, especially in landscape painting and literature. Art forms used in the home, such as pottery, book illustrations, and even buttons, reflected nature themes in highly decorative designs employing fruits, flowers, birds, plant and marine life. Miniature case designs also relied heavily on a profusion of nature themes. From 1844-1850 a rose motif became such a popular case design that it outsold the many other designs available to the case trade. This rose pattern was adopted in about thirty variants (*see* Plates 123-126).

In the range and scope of design in both leather and paper, the industry was ever expanding, from its first simple designs to the later elaborate scenic views, and then on to the ornate floral and other complex designs of the 1850's. The 1840 decade had set the pace for the heavily ornate baroque and fanciful rococo patterns of the fifties.

The advent of the plastic Union case made a vast array of new patterns possible and created a distinct native art form. The new case material was suited for intricate scenic landscape designs, genre subjects, and sculptured effects, as well as traditional design motifs.

Artist-engravers who had produced designs on leather for the case industry were also now cutting designs on steel for the new plastic composition. The art of die-engraving or diesinking (as it was also called) on steel molds was one that the Greeks had refined to the point of perfection. Although it fell into obscurity for a while, it was revived in the sixteenth century when an attempt was made to recapture its ancient glory. In preparing his die, the artist used his metal in a soft state for engraving upon. The process entailed working in reverse, that is, he cut or sank those parts of his design which were rounded in the finished product. He took many impressions in clay of his work as it progressed in order to judge its total effect and to make any necessary corrections. After the steel die was finished, it was hardened by fire—a red heat was necessary; it was then cooled in a small quantity of water where it remained until perfectly cold. This process required extreme care to prevent breakage or splitting. The finished die, having the inverse figure or ornament, could then be struck or cast in relief for any decorative process.[2] The dies for making plastic daguerreotype cases were used in a mold press

which was operated with a powerful screw-type pressure (*see* Figs. 20 and 27).

The dies produced by these artist-engravers truly reflected the increasingly elaborate design influences of the 1850's. Gothic style architecture attained a peak of popularity by the 1850's. Yet the preference for mixed architectural styles made a completely Gothic structure a rarity; "Italianate," a variant of Gothic, was extensively used in America in 1850's. Richly carved and ornamental interior furnishings that reflected seventeenth and eighteenth century European baroque styling, were also a design factor. Mass production of furniture had begun in the 1830's. In 1844 with the invention of the power loom by Bigelow, brightly colored carpets of Gothic pavement and other intricate patterns began to decorate American floors.[3] By 1850, the firmly established home decorating trend was toward the elaborate. Another influence on the design of the day was the work of Robert Adam, famous eighteenth century English architect and furniture designer. And all of Adam's essentially classical designs—medallions, rosettes, delicate acanthus scrolling, festoons of husks, wheat sheaves, and radiating designs—were represented on miniature case covers.

During the three decades before the Civil War religion had experienced an enormous growth. A large immigration to America during the 1840's and '50's increased their number, according to a church historian, from 244,500 in 1820 to 3,000,000 members by 1860. This growth of the Catholic population may have accounted for the revival of interest in Christian art in the pre-Civil War era.[4] A profusion of cross motifs and other religiously smybolic geometric designs on miniature case covers reflect the ancient Christian Art forms. (*see* Plates 53-59).

Death was symbolized in many American art forms such as carvings on grave stones and monuments, and painted memorial scenes. And in the 1840's the infant art of photography popularized the photographing of the dead. By 1850, taking portraits of the departed had become an important part of the daguerreian art. The first plastic daguerreotype case introduced to the public might well have been designed especially to hold portraits of the deceased. An announcement in 1852 in *Humphrey's Journal,* a photography publication, noted that the Scovill Manufacturing Company carried a new and beautiful case, "for the likenesses of deceased persons, and for all sepulchral daguerreotypes—for which purpose they are peculiarly adapted. The designs are unique, the whole appropriate—rich without being gaudy."[5] Other casemakers obviously adopted designs suitable for cases made to hold portraits of the dead (*see* Plates 60-65); a New York business directory of 1856 listed a manufacturer with the name Mausoleum Daguerreotype Case Co.[6]

In sharp contrast to the death theme, case covers depicted light-hearted and sentimental subjects in the form of highly romantic representations of scenes and people. These lithograph-type designs, reminiscent of the style of Currier and Ives, showed fictional characters from nursery rhymes, scenes from poetry and literature, mythological themes of ancient origins. Important scenes in American history, which had been painted on canvas by native artists were copied; historical scenes and portraits from other lands were also pictured by the die-engravers.

Before and during the Civil War many designs on plastic, paper, and cloth began assuming a nationalistic flavor. Several designs on cases of the early 1860's, both plastic and cloth-covered, showed a symbolic representation of the spirit of war times (see Plates 66-79).

Unfortunately, there exists no precise written record summarizing the development of plastic case designs from beginning to end. The only inkling of an early pattern was set down in a brief article in a photography journal of 1858:

Now 7 years since Union case introduced . . . one of the first and best patterns being a sixth size with two pretty jolly-faced little girls; afterward very many patterns introduced, varying from senselessly ugly to neatness of design, some as slightly embossed as if the material were of gold, and the maker were afraid of wasting it, others so bold as if intended for distant observations or bases of columns. After some flourishes of prettiness of design came the literary period, with sharp-featured Sir Roger De Coverly, a libel on Addison's hero, The Appointment, some family and domestic scenes, and good and bad, interspersed with the short-lived mania for chequered patterns, which the makers would persist in sending, and people in not liking. After which were issued some really choice and elegant designs—a credit to the purpose for which they were used. Now, we have the historical period. The history of the U. S. is being impressed on the rising generation and it is furbishing up the memories of sober citizens, from the covers of daguerreotype cases. We have Marion sharing his mess of sweet potatoes with a British officer, The Capture of Major André, Washington Crossing the Delaware on a whole size case, etc. The material is admirably adapted for the purpose, and let us hope the manufacture will preserve, only asking them to have purity of design, and no exaggeration of nature.[7]

The manufacturers did indeed continue to produce designs worthy of the art by employing the finest possible artists. Their rich heritage of designs, both in leather and plastic, boasts a greater variety than any other nineteenth century craft. Although many patterns may have been merely faithful copies from contemporary art sources, most designs demonstrate a freshness and originality totally unexpected from this short-lived art form.

PART II

Decorative Art Case Designs

Plates: The History and Sentiments of a People

Plate 1   *Courtesy of Pro-Phy-Lac-Tic Brush Co.*

THE LANDING OF COLUMBUS

Casemaker: Attributed S. Peck and Co.
Plastic, 9⅚₆″ X 7⅚₆″, C. 1858
Die-engraver, F. B. Smith & Hartmann
From a painting by John Vanderlyn

Plate 2   *Coll. of Miss Josephine Cobb*

INDIAN PROFILE

Casemaker: Holmes, Booth & Hayden
Plastic, 2½″ X 3″, C. 1860

WASHINGTON CROSSING THE DELAWARE

Casemaker: Littlefield, Parsons & Co.
Plastic, 9⅛″ X 7³⁄₁₆″, C. 1857
Die-engraver, F. B. Smith & Hartmann
From a painting by Emanuel Leutze

Plate 3

THE ENGLISH PIONEERS

Casemaker: Littlefield, Parsons & Co.
Plastic, 6⅛″ X 5″, C. 1859
Die-engraver, A. Schaefer

THE CAPTURE OF MAJOR ANDRÉ

Casemaker: S. Peck and Co. (Peck and Halvorson's patent)
Plastic, 4″ X 5″, C. 1856
From a painting by Asher B. Durand
Die-engraver, F. Goll

THE MEDALLION OF GEORGE WASHINGTON

Casemaker: S. Peck and Co. (Peck and Halvorson's patent)
Plastic, 3⅜″ X 3¾″, C. 1856
From sculpture by Houdon
Die-engraver, F. Goll

THE WASHINGTON MONUMENT, RICHMOND, VA.

Casemaker: Attributed S. Peck and Co.
Plastic, 4⅛″ X 4″, C. 1858
Die-engraver, F. Goll

THE WASHINGTON MONUMENT, RICHMOND, VA.

Casemaker: Attributed S. Peck and Co.
Plastic, 6¼″ X 5″, C. 1860
Die-engraver, F. Goll

58

Plate 9

THE MONUMENT

Casemaker: Unknown
Leather, 5⅞″ X 4⅝″, C. 1853

Plate 10

THE CLIPPER SHIP AND FORT

Casemaker: Littlefield, Parsons & Co.
Plastic, 3⅜″ X 3¾″, C. 1860
(Cover only, see Nesting Birds for bottom of case)

Plate 11

SEATED LIBERTY

Casemaker: Littlefield, Parsons & Co.
Plastic, 3⅜″ X 3¾″, C. 1858

Plate 12   *Coll. Emerick Hanzl, Jr.*

THE FIRE CHIEF

Casemaker: Littlefield, Parsons & Co.
Plastic, 3¼″ X 3¾″, C. 1858
Die-engraver, A. Schaefer

Plate 13

FIREMAN SAVING CHILD

Casemaker: Littlefield, Parsons & Co.
Plastic, 3¾″ X 3⅜″, C. 1858

Plate 14   *Coll. of Frederick Reehl*

THE WHEAT SHEAVES

Casemaker: Scovill Manufacturing Co.
Plastic, 2½″ X 3″, C. 1860
Die-engraver, F. Key

Plate 15

COUNTRY LIFE

Casemaker: A. P. Critchlow & Co.
Plastic, 5″ X 6⅛″, C. 1858

Plate 17

WOLFERT'S ROOST

Casemaker: Unknown
Leather, 3⅛″ X 3⅝″, C. 1853

Plate 16

THE TRYST (THE APPOINTMENT)

Casemaker: A. P. Critchlow & Co.
Plastic, 4″ X 5″, C. 1857
Die-engraver, A. Schaefer

Plate 18   *Courtesy of The New York Historical Society,*
New York City

A COUNTRY SCENE

Casemaker: Unknown
Leather, 3⅛″ X 3⅝″, C. 1853

Plate 19

YOUNG FARM COUPLE

Casemaker: Littlefield, Parsons & Co.
Plastic, 3″ X 2½″, C. 1858

Plate 20

THE BEEHIVE WITH GRAIN BORDER

Casemaker: Littlefield, Parsons & Co. (attributed)
Plastic, 2½″ X 3″, C. 1859

Plate 21

THE BEEHIVE WITH FRUIT BORDER

Casemaker: Littlefield, Parsons & Co.
Plastic, 2⅝″ X 3″, C. 1859

Plate 22   *Coll. of Mrs. Janie Wright*

THE APPLE PICKER

Casemaker: Littlefield, Parsons & Co.
Plastic, 3½″ X 3⅞″, C. 1858

THE DIAMOND MOTIF

Casemaker: A. B. Chapman
Inlaid mother-of-pearl on wood frame,
3⅛″ X 3⅝″, C. 1870
Courtesy of Time-Out Antiques, N.Y.

ARABESQUE MOTIF

Casemaker: Unknown
Leather, 3⅝″ X 3⅛″, C. 1858

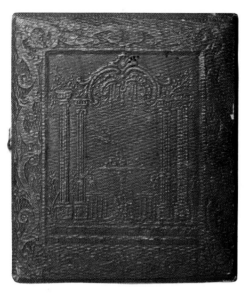

A GARDEN SCENE

Casemaker: Unknown
Leather, 3⅝″ X 3⅛″, C. 1852

COLONIAL GARDEN SCENE

Casemaker: Unknown
Molded plastic on papier-mâché, 3¾″ X 3⅜″, C. 1855

Collection of Miss Josephine Cobb

SPRAY OF FLOWERS, VARIANT

Casemaker: Unknown
Papier-mâché, 3⅞″ X 3½″, C. 1856
Inlaid mother-of-pearl

THE THREE ROSES

Casemaker: Unknown
Papier-mâché, 3⅞″ X 3½″, C. 1851
Inlaid mother-of-pearl

MOUNTAIN SCENE

Casemaker: Unknown
Papier-mâché, 4″ X 3½″, C. 1852
Hand painted, inlaid mother-of-pearl

SPRAY OF FLOWERS, VARIANT

Casemaker: Unknown
Papier-mâché, 4″ X 3⅜″, C. 1850
Inlaid mother-of-pearl

THE LILY MOTIF

Casemaker: Unknown
Leather, 3⅝″ X 3⅛″, C. 1856

Plate 24

CATCHING BUTTERFLIES

Casemaker: Littlefield, Parsons & Co.
Plastic, 2½″ X 3″, C. 1861

Plate 23   *Coll. of Emerick Hanzl, Jr.*

GOING TO MARKET

Casemaker: Holmes, Booth & Hayden
Plastic, 2½″ X 3″, C. 1860

Plate 26

MARY AND HER LAMB

Casemaker: Littlefield, Parsons & Co.
Plastic, 2½″ X 3″, C. 1861

Plate 25   Coll. of J. Harry Du Bois

BOBBY SHAFTO

Casemaker: A. P. Critchlow & Co.
Plastic, 3¾″ X 3¼″, C. 1857

66

Plate 27

THE BLIND BEGGAR

Casemaker: Littlefield, Parsons & Co.
Plastic, 2⅝″ X 3″, C. 1860

Plate 28   *Coll. of Emerick Hanzl, Jr.*

THE MUSICIANS

Casemaker: Littlefield, Parsons & Co.
Plastic, 3¼″ X 3¾″, C. 1859
Die-engraver, A. Schaefer

Plate 29   *Coll. of Emerick Hanzl, Jr.*

CHILDREN PLAYING WITH TOYS

Casemaker: Littlefield, Parsons & Co.
Plastic, 3″ X 4⅝″, C. 1860
A double picture case.

Plate 30   *Coll. of J. Harry Du Bois*

SEATED WOMAN HOLDING CHILD AND PETS

Casemaker: Littlefield, Parsons & Co.
Plastic, 4⅝″ X 3″, C. 1859

67

Plate 31   *Coll. of Frederick Reehl*

THE COUNTRY DANCE

Casemaker: S. Peck and Co.
Plastic, 4¼″ X 5″, C. 1856
Die-engraver, F. B. Smith & Hartmann

Plate 32

THE ARTS

Casemaker: Unknown
Leather, 3⅝″ X 3⅛″, C. 1855

Plate 33

THE SAILBOAT

Casemaker: Unknown
Leather, 3⅝″ X 3½″, C. 1847

Plate 34

THE HORSE RACE

Casemaker: S. Peck and Co. (Peck and Halvorson's patent)
Plastic, 4¼″ X 5″, C. 1856
Die-engraver, F. Goll

Plate 35

CUPID AND THE WOUNDED STAG

Casemaker: A. P. Critchlow & Co.
Plastic, 5″ X 4″, C. 1856

Plate 36   *Coll. of Mrs. Janie Wright*

CUPID AND THE WOUNDED STAG, VARIANT

Casemaker: Littlefield, Parsons & Co.
Plastic, 3⁵⁄₁₆″ X 3⅞″, C. 1862*

Plate 37   *Coll. of Mrs. Janie Wright*

EGYPTIAN WOMEN AND BABY

Casemaker: Littlefield, Parsons & Co.
Plastic, 2¾₁₆″ X 2⅝″, C. 1865

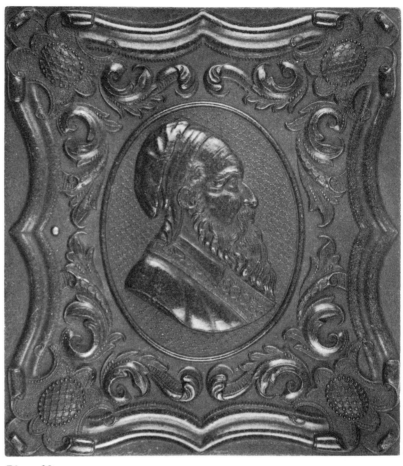

Plate 38

PROFILE OF A PATRIARCH

Casemaker: S. Peck and Co.
Plastic, 3⅞″ X 3½″, C. 1857
Die-engraver, J. Smith

Plate 39

THE MEDITATING MONK

Casemaker: Littlefield, Parsons & Co.
Plastic, 1⅞″ X 2⅛″, C. 1860

Plate 41

THE CHESS PLAYERS

Casemaker: Littlefield, Parsons & Co.
Plastic, 3⅜″ X 3¾″, C. 1860

Plate 40

THE FAITHFUL HOUND

Casemaker: Littlefield, Parsons & Co.
Plastic, 3⅞″ X 6¼″, C. 1858

Plate 42

THE CALMADY CHILDREN

Casemaker: S. Peck and Co.
Plastic, 5″ X 4⅛″, C. 1853
Die-engraver, Hiram W. Hayden
From painting by Sir Thomas Lawrence

Plate 43

THE GYPSY FORTUNE TELLER

Casemaker: A. P. Critchlow & Co.
Plastic, 4⅛″ X 5″, C. 1857

Plate 44

THE HUNTRESS AND THE FALCON

Casemaker: A. P. Critchlow & Co.
Plastic, 3¾″ X 3⅛″, C. 1856
Die-engraver, A. Schaefer

Plate 45   *Courtesy of The New York Historical Society,*
New York City

THE HIGHLAND HUNTER

Casemaker: Holmes, Booth & Hayden
Plastic, 3⅜″ X 3¾″, C. 1859

SIR HENRY HAVELOCK

Casemaker: Littlefield, Parsons & Co.
Plastic, 4⅞″ X 4″, C. 1860

Plate 47   *Coll. of J. Harry Du Bois*

THE HOLY FAMILY

Casemaker: Probably Henning & Eymann
Plastic, 6⅛″ X 5″, C. 1860
Die-engraver, Henning & Eymann

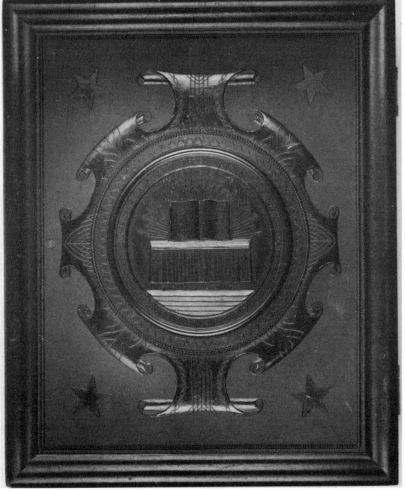

Plate 48

THE LORD'S PRAYER

Casemaker: S. Peck and Co.
Plastic, 5″ X 4¼″, C. 1853
(Rear cover of "The Memorial")

76

ANGEL WITH TRUMPET   **ANGEL SCATTERING ROSES**

Casemaker: Littlefield, Parsons & Co.   Casemaker: S. Peck and Co.
Plastic, 3″ X 2½″, C. 1857   Plastic, 3″ X 2½″, C. 1856

Plate 51

ANGEL CARRYING BABIES

Casemaker: S. Peck and Co. (Peck and Halvorson's patent)
Plastic, 3″ X 2½″, C. 1856

Plate 52

THE CHURCH WINDOW

Casemaker: A. P. Critchlow and Co.
Plastic, 3″ X 2½″, C. 1857

78

Plate 53

THE CROSS PATEE, VARIATION

Casemaker: Unknown
Paper, 2⅜″ X 2⅞″, C. 1862

Plate 54

TOULOUSE CROSS, VARIATION

Casemaker: Unknown
Paper, 2¼″ X 2¾″, C. 1862

Plate 55

THE CROSS PATEE, VARIATION, GRAPE MOTIF

Casemaker: Scovill Manufacturing Co.
Plastic, 3″ X 2½″, C. 1861
Die-engraver, F. Key

Plate 56

THE CROSS MOTIF WITH SCROLL BORDER

Casemaker: Scovill Manufacturing Co.
Plastic, 3¾″ X 3⅜″, C. 1862
Die-engraver, F. Key

80

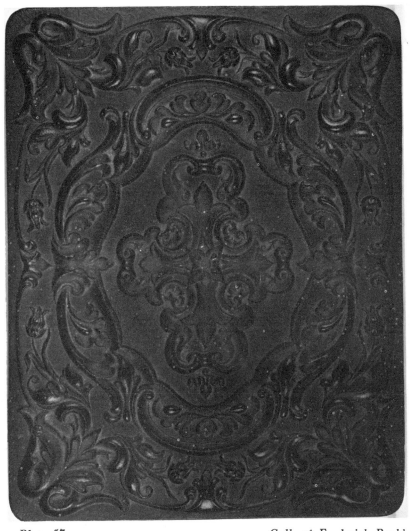

Plate 57   *Coll. of Frederick Reehl*

THE ORNATE CROSS, FLEUR-DE-LIS

Casemaker: Scovill Manufacturing Co.
Plastic, 4″ X 5″, C. 1861

Plate 58

THE CROSS PATEE, VARIATION WITH FLOWER BORDER

Casemaker: Scovill Manufacturing Co.
Plastic, 3¾″ X 3⅜″, C. 1860
Die-engraver, F. Key

Plate 59

THE CROSS AND THE CANDLES

Casemaker: Unknown
Leather, 3⅛″ X 3⅝″, C. 1848

Plate 60

THE LAUNCHING

Casemaker: Probably F. Goll
Plastic, 3½″ X 3⅞″, C. 1856
Die-engraver, F. Goll

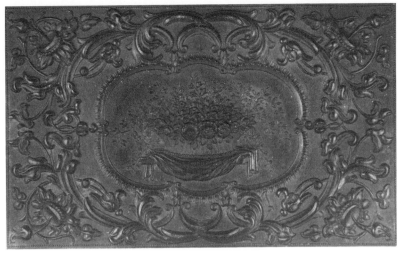

Plate 61

THE FLOWER BIER

Casemaker: Littlefield, Parsons & Co.
Plastic, 3¾″ X 6¼″, C. 1859

Plate 62

THE MEMORIAL

Casemaker: S. Peck and Co.
Plastic, 5″ X 4¼″, C. 1853
Die-engraver, R. Paine

Plate 63

THE LYRE MEMORIAL

Casemaker: Unknown
Leather, 6″ X 4¾″, C. 1854

Plate 64

THE EVERLASTING LIGHT

Casemaker: Unknown
Leather, 3⅝″ X 3⅛″, C. 1856

Plate 65

THE ALTAR MEMORIAL

Casemaker: Unknown
Leather, 2⅛″ X 2⅜″, C. 1854

84

Plate 66

THE FLAG IN GOLD

Casemaker: Unknown
Cardboard, 3⅝″ X 3⅛″, C. 1862

Plate 67

LIBERTY AND THE FLAG

Casemaker: Unknown
Paper, 3⅝″ X 3⅛″, C. 1863

Plate 68

THE FIGHTING EAGLE

Casemaker: Unknown
Paper, 2⅞″ X 2⅜″, C. 1862

Plate 69

THE EAGLE IN FLIGHT

Casemaker: Unknown
Leather, 3⅝″ X 3⅛″, C. 1859

Plate 70

THE EAGLE AT BAY

Casemaker: Littlefield, Parsons & Co.
Plastic, 3¾″ X 3⅜″, C. 1862

Plate 71

THE MONITOR AND FORT

Casemaker: Littlefield, Parsons & Co.
Plastic, 3⅜″ X 3¾″, C. 1863

Plate 72

THE MONITOR AND FORT, VARIANT

Casemaker: Littlefield, Parsons & Co.
Plastic, 2½″ X 3″, C. 1863

Plate 73   *Coll. of Emerick Hanzl, Jr.*

THE SHIP'S STERN

Casemaker: Littlefield, Parsons & Co.
Plastic, 2½″ X 3″, C. 1862

Plate 74   *Coll. of Emerick Hanzl, Jr.*

A SAILOR WITH TELESCOPE

Casemaker: Littlefield, Parsons & Co.
Plastic, 2⅛″ X 1⅞″, C. 1863

Plate 75   *Coll. of Emerick Hanzl, Jr.*

THE UNION AND CONSTITUTION

Casemaker: Littlefield, Parsons & Co.
Plastic, 2½″ X 3″, C. 1861

Plate 76   *Coll. of Emerick Hanzl, Jr.*

THE SCROLL, CONSTITUTION, AND THE LAWS

Casemaker: Littlefield, Parsons & Co.
Plastic, 3¼″ X 3¾″, C. 1862

89

THE CROSSED CANNONS

Casemaker: S. Peck and Co.
Plastic, 3⅜″ X 3¾″, C. 1861

UNION FOREVER

Casemaker: Littlefield, Parsons & Co.
Plastic, 2½″ X 3″, C. 1862

90

Plate 79   *Coll. Emerick Hanzl, Jr.*

THE CAMP SCENE

Casemaker: Littlefield, Parsons & Co.
Plastic, 2½″ X 3″, C. 1863

Plates: Nature Themes

Plate 80

A GARDEN SCENE

Casemaker: Unknown
Leather, 3⅛″ X 3⅝″, C. 1852

Plate 81

DEER AT REST

Casemaker: Unknown
Leather, 3⅝″ X 3⅛″, C. 1851

Plate 82

THE PROUD ELK

Casemaker: Probably Littlefield, Parsons & Co.
Plastic, 3⅜″ X 3¾″, C. 1860
Die-engraver, Smith

Plate 83

THE NESTING SWAN

Casemaker: Unknown
Leather, 3⅝″ X 3⅛″, C. 1849

96

Plate 84

THE NESTING BIRDS

Casemaker: Littlefield, Parsons & Co.
Plastic, 3¼″ X 3¾″, C. 1860

Plate 85

BIRDS ON A RING

Casemaker: Unknown
Cloth, 3⅝″ X 3⅛″, C. 1859

Plate 86

LOVE BIRDS

Casemaker: Unknown
Leather, 3⅝″ X 3⅛″, C. 1851

Plate 87

THE HUMMINGBIRD

Casemaker: Unknown
Leather, 2⅞″ X 2⅜″, C. 1854

98

Plate 88   *Coll. of Mrs. Janie Wright*

BIRDS AND FLOWERS

Casemaker: Unknown
Plastic, 3⅞″ X 3⅜″, C. 1858

Plate 89

THE BIRD AND THE GRAPE VINE

Casemaker: Unknown
Leather, 3⅝″ X 3⅛″, C. 1854

99

Plate 90

THE BIRD AND THE GRAPE VINE, VARIANT

Casemaker: Unknown
Leather, 3⅝″ X 3⅛″, C. 1855

100

Plate 91

BIRDS AND FLOWER VASE

Casemaker: Unknown
Leather, 3⅝″ X 3⅛″, C. 1856

Plate 93

BIRDS AND THE FOUNTAIN

Casemaker: Unknown
Leather, 3⅝″ X 3⅛″, C. 1857
(Plastic variant exists of this design)

Plate 92

BIRDS AND FLOWER BASKET

Casemaker: Unknown
Leather, 3⅝″ X 3⅛″, C. 1853

Plate 95

THE HOVERING BIRD, VARIANT

Casemaker: Unknown
Leather, 3⅛″ X 3⅝″, C. 1857

Plate 94

THE HOVERING BIRD

Casemaker: Unknown
Leather, 2⅞″ X 2⅜″, C. 1854

Plate 96

BIRD AND SNAKE

Casemaker: Unknown
Leather, 3⅝″ X 3⅛″, C. 1855

Plate 97

WATER BIRD AND THE URN

Casemaker: Unknown
Leather, 3½″ X 3″, C. 1850

Plate 98

THE DELUGE

Casemaker: Unknown
Leather, 3⅝″ X 3⅛″, C. 1856

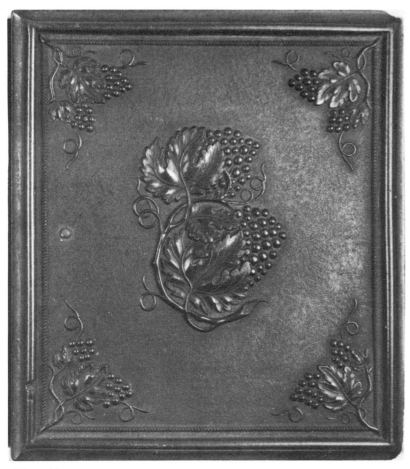

Plate 99

THE BERRY MOTIF

Casemaker: S. Peck and Co,
Plastic, 3½″ X 3⅞″, C. 1858

Plate 100

THE DELICATE GRAPES

Casemaker: Unknown
Leather, 3⅝″ X 3⅛″, C. 1847

Plate 101

WREATH OF GRAPES

Casemaker: Unknown
Plastic, 3⅜″ X 3¾″, C. 1854

Plate 102

THE GRAPE MEDALLION

Casemaker: Unknown
Leather, 3⅝″ X 3⅛″, C. 1857

106

Plate 103

THE FISH AND GRAPE MOTIF

Casemaker: Unknown
Leather, 3⅝″ X 3⅛″, C. 1854

Plate 104

CLUSTER OF CHERRIES

Casemaker: Unknown
Plastic, 2½″ X 3″, C. 1857

STRAWBERRY MOTIF

Casemaker: Littlefield, Parsons & Co.
Plastic, 2½″ X 3″, C. 1859

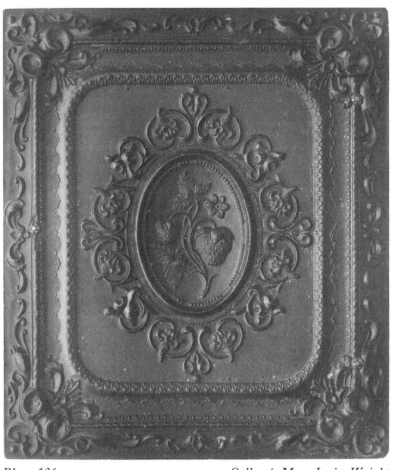

Plate 106   Coll. of Mrs. Janie Wright

TWO STRAWBERRY MOTIF

Casemaker: Probably Littlefield, Parsons & Co.
Plastic, 3⅜″ X 3¾″, C. 1859

Plate 107

THE FRUITED BOUGH

Casemaker: Littlefield, Parsons & Co.
Plastic, 2⅝″ X 2⅛″, C. 1863

Plate 108

VASE WITH FRUITS AND FLOWERS

Casemaker: Unknown
Leather, 4¾″ X 6″, C. 1856

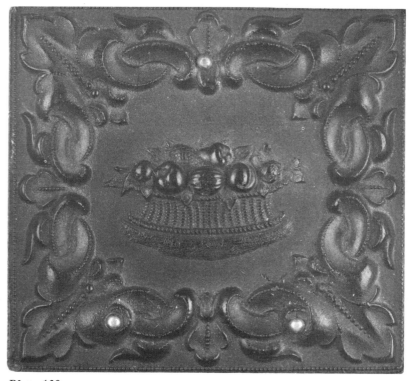

Plate 109

A BASKET OF FRUITS AND VEGETABLES

Casemaker: Holmes, Booth & Hayden
Plastic, 1⅞″ X 2⅛″, C. 1863
Die-engraver, W. E. Houston

Plate 111

FRUITS OF THE HARVEST

Casemaker: Scovill Manufacturing Co.
Plastic, 1⅞″ X 2⅛″, C. 1865

Plate 110   *Coll. of Mrs. Janie Wright*

A BOWL OF FRUIT

Casemaker: Florence Manufacturing Co. (L. P. patent)
Plastic, 4⅞″ X 6⅛″, C. 1868

Plate 112

TWO LILIES

Casemaker: Unknown
Leather, 3⅝″ X 3⅛″, C. 1850

Plate 113

TWO LILIES, VARIANT

Casemaker: Probably E. Anthony and Co.
Leather, 3⅝″ X 3⅛″, C. 1854

Plate 114

LILY AND ROSE

Casemaker: Unknown
Leather, 3⅝″ X 3⅛″, C. 1850

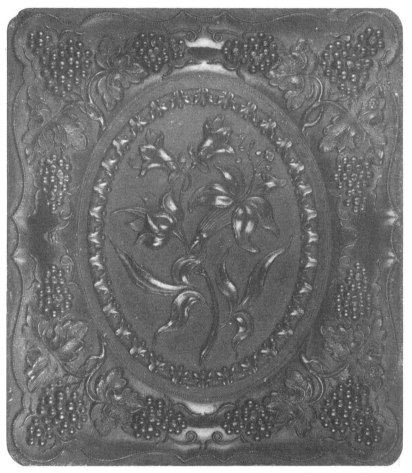

Plate 115   *Coll. of Frederick Reehl*

LILIES AND GRAPES

Casemaker: Scovill Mfg. Co.
Plastic, 2½″ X 3″, C. 1864

113

Plate 116

THE TULIP AND DIAMOND

Casemaker: Unknown
Leather, 3⅝″ X 3⅛″, C. 1849
Die-engraver, David Pretlove

Plate 117

THE MORNING GLORY

Casemaker: Unknown
Leather, 3⅝″ X 3⅛″, C. 1851

Plate 118

THE DANDELION

Casemaker: Unknown
Leather, 3⅝″ X 3⅛″, C. 1853

Plate 119

THISTLE MOTIF

Casemaker: Unknown
Leather, 3⅝″ X 3⅛″, C. 1858

115

Plate 120

MAIDEN SCATTERING ROSES

Casemaker: Unknown
Leather, 3⅝″ X 3⅛″, C. 1854

Plate 121

A TINY GOLDEN ROSE

Casemaker: Unknown
Leather, 3⅛″ X 3⅝″, C. 1848

Plate 122

A SINGLE ROSE

Casemaker: Unknown
Cloth, 4¾″ X 3¾″, C. 1862

Plate 123

THE DELICATE ROSES, VARIANT

Casemaker: Unknown
Leather, 3⅝″ X 3⅛″, C. 1844
Die-engraver, David Pretlove

117

Plate 124

THE DELICATE ROSES, VARIANT

Casemaker: Unknown
Leather, 3⅝" X 3⅛", C. 1845

Plate 125

THE DELICATE ROSES, VARIANT

Casemaker: Unknown
Leather, 3⅝" X 3⅛", C. 1847

Plate 126

ORNATE DELICATE ROSES

Casemaker: Unknown
Leather, 3⅝″ X 3⅛″, C. 1848

Plate 127

A SPRAY OF ROSES, VARIANT

Casemaker: Unknown
Leather, 3⅝″ X 3⅛″, C. 1857

Plate 128

MEDALLION OF THREE ROSES

Casemaker: Unknown
Cloth, 3⅝″ X 3⅛″, C. 1857

Plate 129

THE ROSE CAMEO

Casemaker: Unknown
Papier-mâché, 3⅝″ X 3⅛″, C. 1858

120

Plate 130

THE TEA ROSE

Casemaker: Unknown
Leather, 4¾″ X 3¾″, C. 1851
Die-engraver, David Pretlove

Plate 131

A SPRAY OF ROSES

Casemaker: Unknown
Leather, 3⅝″ X 3⅛″, C. 1851

121

Plate 132

THE BOWER MAIDEN

Casemaker: Unknown
Leather, 3⅝″ X 3⅛″, C. 1848

Plate 133

MIXED GARDEN FLOWERS

Casemaker: Unknown
Leather, 3⅝″ X 3⅛″, C. 1851
Die-engraver, David Pretlove

Plate 134

BOUQUET OF FLOWERS

Casemaker: Unknown
Leather, 3⅝″ X 3⅛″, C. 1851

Plate 135

FLOWER MEDALLION

Casemaker: Unknown
Leather, 3⅝″ X 3⅛″, C. 1854

123

Plate 136

MIXED FLOWERS

Casemaker: Unknown
Leather, 3⅝″ X 3⅛″, C. 1855

Plate 137

MIXED FLOWERS, VARIANT

Casemaker: Unknown
Paper, 3⅝″ X 3⅛″, C. 1857

Plate 138

MIXED FLOWERS, VARIANT

Casemaker: Unknown
Leather, 3⅝″ X 3⅛″, C. 1848
Die-engraver, David Pretlove

Plate 139

SPRAY OF FLOWERS

Casemaker: Unknown
Papier-mâché, 3⅞″ X 3⅜″, C. 1854
Inlaid mother-of-pearl

Plate 140

THE GRECIAN URN

Casemaker: John Plumbe, Jr.
Leather, 3⅛″ X 3⅝″, C. 1841

Plate 141

THE ROMANESQUE URN

Casemaker: Unknown
Leather, 3⅝″ X 3⅛″, C. 1857

Plate 142   *Coll. of Mrs. Janie Wright*

GOBLET WITH FLOWERS

Casemaker: Wadham's Manufacturing Co.
Plastic, 3³⁄₁₆″ X 2¹¹⁄₁₆″, C. 1859

Plate 143

JARDINIERE OF FLOWERS

Casemaker: A. P. Critchlow & Co.
Plastic, 3³⁄₈″ X 3³⁄₄″, C. 1857

Plate 144

THE FLOWER CORNUCOPIA

Casemaker: Unknown
Leather, 3⅝″ X 3⅛″, C. 1849

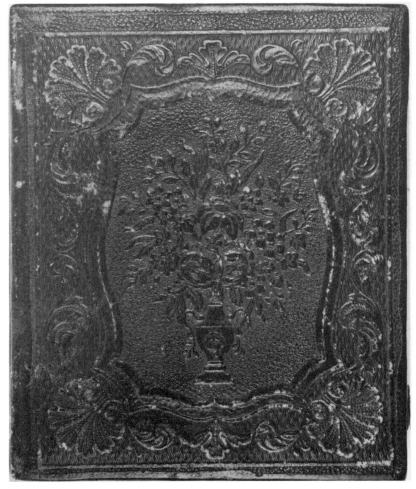

Plate 145

VASE OF FLOWERS

Casemaker: Unknown
Leather, 3⅝″ X 3⅛″, C. 1848

128

Plate 146

FLOWER VASE MOTIF

Casemaker: Unknown
Silk, 3⅝" X 3⅛", C. 1852
Die-engraver: A. C. Paquet

Plate 147   *Coll. of Mrs. Janie Wright*

PEDESTAL VASE WITH ROSES

Casemaker: Littlefield, Parsons & Co.
Plastic, 4⅝" X 3", C. 1863

129

Plate 148

BASKET OF FLOWERS

Casemaker: John Plumbe, Jr.
Leather, 3⅛″ X 3⅝″, C. 1845

Plate 149

BASKET OF FLOWERS, VARIANT

Casemaker: Unknown
Leather, 3⅝″ X 3⅛″, C. 1846

130

Plate 150

NATURE'S BOUQUET

Casemaker: Littlefield, Parsons & Co.
Plastic, 1⅞″ X 2⅛″, C. 1867

Plate 151

MOUNTAIN SCENE

Casemaker: Unknown
Papier-mâché, 4″ X 3½″, C. 1852
Hand painted, inlaid mother-of-pearl border

Plate 152

THE FOUR ACORN MOTIF

Casemaker: Littlefield, Parsons & Co.
Plastic, 3″ X 2½″, C. 1858

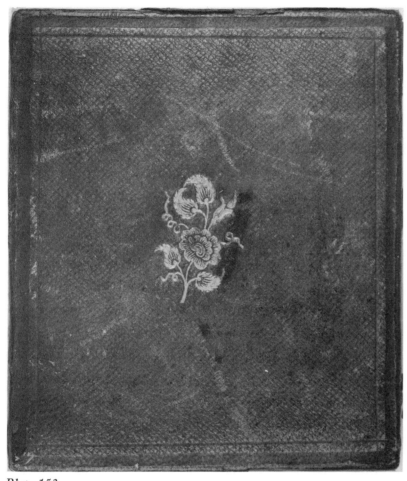

Plate 153

A FLOWER IN GOLD

Casemaker: Unknown
Leather, 3⅝″ X 3⅛″, C. 1854

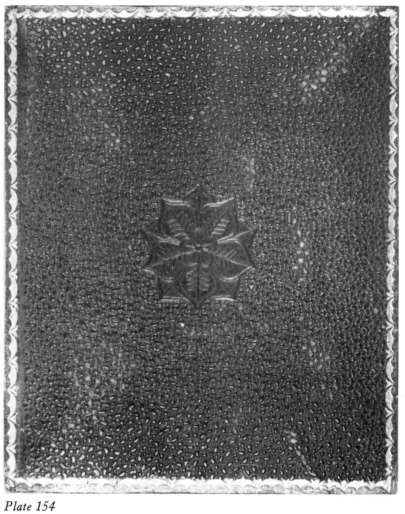

Plate 154

PRESSED FLOWER

Casemaker: Unknown
Leather, 2⅞″ X 2⅜″, C. 1854

133

Plate 155

PICTURE FRAME MOTIF

Casemaker: Unknown
Cardboard, 2⅞" X 2⅜", C. 1865

Plate 156

A FRAME DESIGN

Casemaker: Unknown
Leather, 3⅝" X 3⅛", C. 1857

134

Plate 157

SCALLOP AND FLORAL MOTIF

Casemaker: Unknown
Leather, 3¾" X 1¾", C. 1848

Plate 158

FLORAL SCROLL THEME

Casemaker: S. Peck and Co.
Plastic, 5" X 4⅛", C. 1855

135

Plate 159

A WREATH THEME

Casemaker: A. P. Critchlow & Co.
Plastic, 2½″ X 3″, C. 1856

Plate 160

THE LEAF AND HEART MOTIF

Casemaker: Littlefield, Parsons & Co.
Plastic, 2½″ X 3″, C. 1862

Plate 161

VINE AND ROPE DESIGN

Casemaker: Holmes, Booth & Hayden
Plastic, 2½″ X 3″, C. 1857
Die-engraver, W. E. Houston

137

Plates: Traditional and Geometric Designs

Plate 162

THE CROCKET THEME

Casemaker: Unknown
Leather, 3⅛″ X 3⅝″, C. 1840

Plate 163

MAIDEN WITH CORNUCOPIA

Casemaker: Unknown
Leather, 3⅝″ X 3⅛″, C. 1851

141

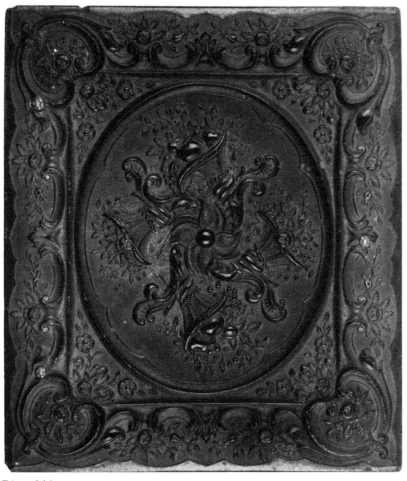

Plate 164

THE WHEEL OF CORNUCOPIAS

Casemaker: Littlefield, Parsons & Co.
Plastic, 3¾″ X 3⅜″, C. 1863

Plate 165

EGYPTIAN MOTIF

Casemaker: Unknown
Leather, 3⅝″ X 3⅛″, C. 1841

142

Plate 166

THE SPEAR AND ROD

Casemaker: Unknown
Leather, 3⅝" X 3⅛", C. 1842

Plate 167

TORCH WITH BOW AND ARROWS

Casemaker: Unknown
Leather, 3¾" X 4¾", C. 1848

Plate 168

THE BELT AND BUCKLE

Casemaker: S. Peck and Co.
Plastic, 3¾″ X 3⅜″, C. 1858

Plate 169   *Coll. of Mrs. Janie Wright*

CHAIN AND BUCKLE

Casemaker: Littlefield, Parsons & Co.
Plastic, 3⁵⁄₁₆″ X 3¾″, C. 1860

144

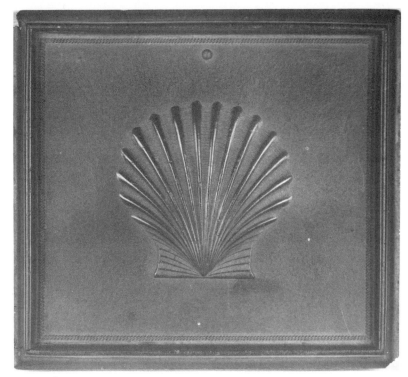

Plate 171

SCALLOP SHELL

Casemaker: S. Peck and Co.
Plastic, 3½″ X 3⅞″, C. 1855

Plate 170

SHIELD AND SHELLS

Casemaker: A. P. Critchlow & Co.
Plastic, 3¾″ X 3⅜″, C. 1857

Plate 172

LYRE MOTIF

Casemaker: Unknown
Leather, 3⅛″ X 3⅝″, C. 1843

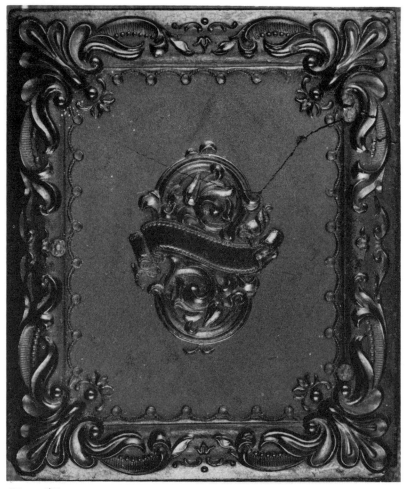

Plate 173

THE RIBBON MOTIF

Casemaker: Littlefield, Parsons & Co.
Plastic, 2½″ X 3″, C. 1860

Plate 174

FORGET ME NOT

Casemaker: Unknown
Leather, 3⅝″ X 4⅝″, C. 1855
Die-engraver: C. Loekle

146

Plate 175

THE LOVING CUP

Casemaker: Unknown
Cardboard, 2⅞″ X 2⅜″, C. 1861

Plate 176   *Coll. of Miss Josephine Cobb*

THE CAMEO

Casemaker: S. Peck and Co.
Plastic, 3⅜″ X 3¾″, C. 1857

Plate 177

THE PRECIOUS STONE

Casemaker: S. Peck and Co. (attributed)
Plastic, 3⅜″ X 3¾″, C. 1855

Plate 178

JEWEL MOTIF

Casemaker: Littlefield, Parsons & Co.
Plastic, 3⅜″ X 3¾″, C. 1859

Plate 179

LITTLE GEM

Casemaker: Littlefield, Parsons & Co.
Plastic, 3¾″ X 3⅜″, C. 1859

149

Plate 180

STAR SAPPHIRE MOTIF

Casemaker: Littlefield, Parsons & Co.
Plastic, 3″ X 2⅝″, C. 1859

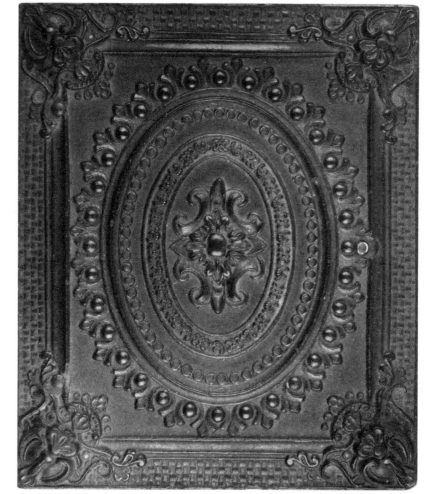

Plate 181

PEARL MOTIF

Casemaker: S. Peck and Co. (no patent label)
Plastic, 2½″ X 3″, C. 1859*

150

Plate 183

ORNATE SCROLL MOTIF

Casemaker: S. Peck and Co. (unmarked)
Plastic, 3⅛″ X 2⅝″, C. 1854

Plate 182

LILY SCROLL MOTIF

Casemaker: Littlefield, Parsons & Co.
Plastic, 3¾″ X 3⅜″, C. 1860

Plate 184

SCROLL DESIGN WITH DIAPERED CENTER

Casemaker: S. Peck and Co.
Plastic, 3⅛″ X 2⅝″, C. 1855

Plate 185

SCROLL AND LEAF DESIGN

Casemaker: Unknown
Leather, 3⅝″ X 3⅛″, C. 1846*

152

Plate 186

LINK AND SCROLL MOTIF WITH DIAPERED CENTER

Casemaker: Unmarked (probably S. Peck and Co.)
Plastic, 3½″ X 3⅞″, C. 1857

Plate 187

SCROLL MOTIF WITH GEOMETRIC BORDER

Casemaker: Unknown
Leather, 3⅛″ X 3⅝″, C. 1847*

Plate 188

THE KEYHOLE MOTIF

Casemaker: Littlefield, Parsons & Co.
Plastic, 2⅝″ X 3″, C. 1863

Plate 189

AN EIGHT SCROLL ROSETTE

Casemaker: S. Peck and Co.
Plastic, 2⅝″ X 3⅛″, C. 1855

154

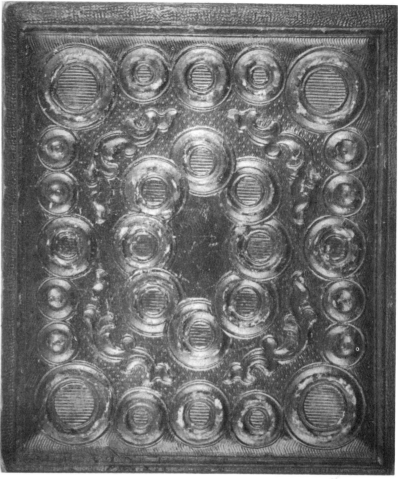

Plate 191

THE AMULETS

Casemaker: Unknown
Cardboard, 3⅝″ X 3⅛″, C. 1861

Plate 190   *Coll. of Mrs. Janie Wright*

THE GOLDEN DISK

Casemaker: S. Peck and Co.
Plastic, 4$\frac{3}{16}$″ X 5$\frac{1}{16}$″, C. 1857

Plate 192

THE DOTTED CIRCLE

Casemaker: Littlefield, Parsons & Co.
Plastic, 3¾″ X 3⅜″, C. 1860

Plate 193

A CIRCLE MOTIF

Casemaker: Unknown
Leather, 3⅝″ X 3⅛″, C. 1841

Plate 194

THE ROSETTE MOTIF

Casemaker: S. Peck and Co.
Plastic, 3½" X 3⅞", C. 1854

Plate 195

THE TANGENT CIRCLE

Casemaker: Unknown
Leather, 3⅝" X 3⅛", C. 1852

157

Plate 196

ORNAMENTAL CIRCLE THEME

Casemaker: Unknown
Cloth, 3⅝″ X 3⅛″, C. 1862

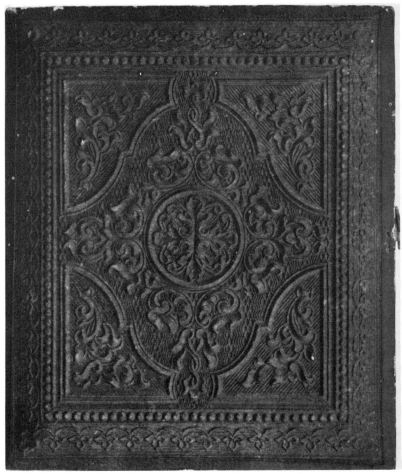

Plate 197

LEAF CIRCLE MOTIF

Casemaker: Unknown
Cardboard, 3⅝″ X 3⅛″, C. 1859

Plate 198

THE OVAL, DIAMOND AND CIRCLE

Casemaker: Unknown
Leather, 2⅞″ X 2⅜″, C. 1851

Plate 199

CURVED DIAMOND

Casemaker: Unknown
Leather, 3⁵⁄₁₀″ X 3¹⁄₀″, C. 1842

Plate 200

TEN POINT STAR

Casemaker: S. Peck and Co.
Plastic, 3⅞″ X 3½″, C. 1856
Die-engraver, J. Smith

Plate 201

THE WOVEN STARS

Casemaker: Unknown
Leather, 3⅝″ X 3⅛″, C. 1860

160

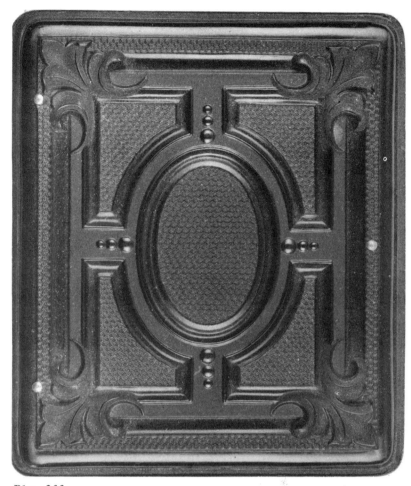

Plate 203

CONVENTIONAL OVAL MOTIF

Casemaker: Littlefield, Parsons & Co.
Plastic, 3⅜″ X 3¾″, C. 1859

Plate 202

MONOGRAM MOTIF

Casemaker: Littlefield, Parsons & Co.
Plastic, 3¾″ X 3⅜″, C. 1859

161

Plate 204

OVAL MOTIF WITH DIAPERED CENTER

Casemaker: Holmes, Booth & Hayden
Plastic, 3⅜″ X 3¾″, C. 1863

Plate 205

ACCENTED OVAL

Casemaker: S. Peck and Co. (Peck and Halvorson Patent)
Plastic, 3¾″ X 3⅜″, C. 1857
Die-engraver, Smith

162

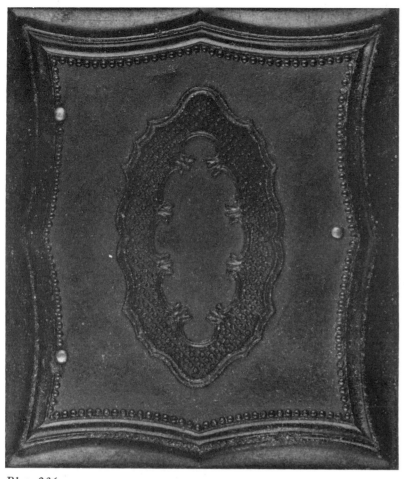

Plate 206

SCALLOPED OVAL

Casemaker: A. P. Critchlow & Co.
Plastic, 3″ X 2½″, C. 1857

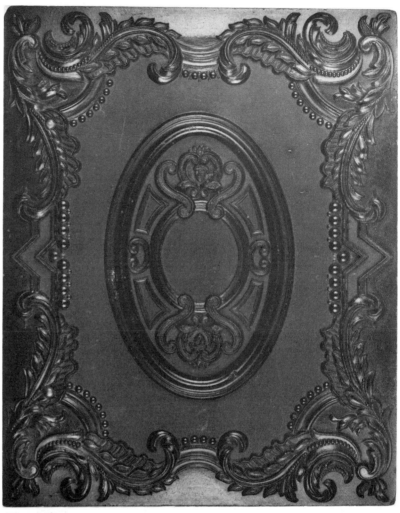

Plate 207

THE TINY HEADS IN OVAL

Casemaker: Unknown
Plastic, 5″ X 4″, C. 1857

163

Plate 208

FRENCH PROVINCIAL

Casemaker: Scovill Mfg. Co. (Attributed)
Plastic, 5″ X 4″, C. 1861
Die-engraver, Frederick Key

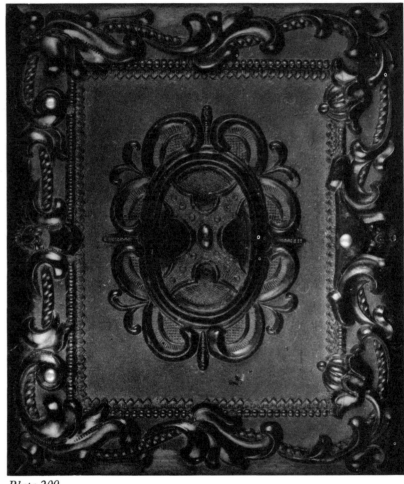

Plate 209

THE CARVED OVAL

Casemaker: Holmes, Booth & Hayden
Plastic, 3″ X 2½″, C. 1858

Plate 210

THE FOUR POINTS

Casemaker: Unknown
Leather, 2⅞″ X 2⅜″, C. 1857

Plate 211

CARVED OVAL MOTIF

Casemaker: Unknown
Paper and leather, 3⅝″ X 3⅛″, C. 1853

Plate 212

THE FLOWER QUATREFOIL

Casemaker: S. Peck and Co.
Plastic, 4⅛″ X 5″, C. 1854
Die-engraver, Frederick Key

Plate 213

MOORISH DESIGN

Casemaker; A. P. Critchlow & Co.
Plastic, 3¾″ X 3⅜″, C. 1857

166

Plate 214

THE FIVE DIAMONDS

Casemaker: Unknown
Paper, 4⅝" X 3¾", C. 1864

Plate 215

SUNBURST MOTIF

Casemaker: A. P. Critchlow & Co.
Plastic, 3" X 2⅝", C. 1857

167

Plate 216   *Coll. of Frederick Reehl*

THE VALENTINE

Casemaker: Littlefield, Parsons & Co.
Plastic, 3⅜″ X 3¾″, C. 1859

Plate 217

THE CURVED OCTAGON

Casemaker: Unknown
Leather, 3⅝" X 3⅛", C. 1847

Plate 218

THE PLAIN OCTAGON

Casemaker: Unknown
Leather, 3⅛" X 3⅝", C. 1844

169

Plate 219

CURVED OCTAGON WITH SCROLL CENTER MOTIF

Casemaker: William Shew
Leather, 3⅛″ X 3⅝″, C. 1845

Plate 220

LINK DESIGN

Casemaker: S. Peck and Co. (Attributed)
Plastic, 2⅝″ X 3⅛″, C. 1854
Die-engraver, Smith

Plate 221

THE HEXAGON ROSETTE

Casemaker: Scovill Mfg. Co.
Plastic, 3″ X 2½″, C. 1861
Die-engraver, Frederick Key

Plate 223

THE MAGNIFIED CIRCLE MOTIF

Casemaker: S. Peck and Co.
Plastic, 3½″ X 3⅞″, C. 1856

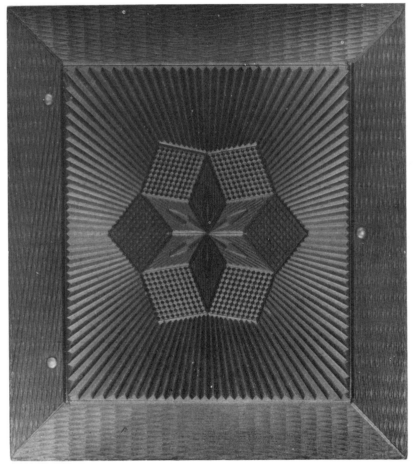

Plate 222   *Coll. of Mrs. Janie Wright*

THE CHANGEABLE CUBES

Casemaker: A. P. Critchlow & Co.
Plastic, 3½″ X 3⅞″, C. 1856

Plate 224

THE RING

Casemaker: Unknown
Cardboard, 2⅞″ X 2⅜″, C. 1857

Plate 225

CUT GLASS MOTIF

Casemaker: Unknown
Cardboard, 3⅝″ X 3⅛″, C. 1853

Plate 226

ORIENTAL MOTIF

Casemaker: Unknown
Leather, 3⅝″ X 3⅛″, C. 1853

Plate 227

ARABESQUE MOTIF

Casemaker: Unknown
Leather, 3⅝″ X 3⅛″, C. 1858

Plate 228

THE INTERLACED SPIRALS

Casemaker: Unknown
Leather, 3⅝″ X 3⅛″, C. 1845

Plate 229

THE STRAWBERRY BORDER

Casemaker: Unknown
Leather, 3⅛″ X 3⅝″, C. 1851

175

Appendix

COMPARISON CHARTS ON THE STANDARD MINIATURE CASE MANUFACTURED FOR EARLY PHOTOGRAPHY (1839-1870)

TABLE No. 1   A chart of the standard photographic Plate measurement and the miniature case used by each size.

Standard name used by photography and casemakers to denote size	Standard pioneer photographic plate measurement[1]	A general outside measurement of the leather case
Whole (size)	$6\frac{1}{2}$ x $8\frac{1}{2}$ inches	7 x $9\frac{1}{8}$ inches
Half "	$4\frac{1}{2}$ x $5\frac{1}{2}$ "	$4\frac{7}{8}$ x 6 "
Quarter "	$3\frac{1}{4}$ x $4\frac{1}{4}$ "	$3\frac{3}{4}$ x $4\frac{3}{4}$ "
Sixth "	$2\frac{3}{4}$ x $3\frac{1}{4}$ "	$3\frac{1}{8}$ x $3\frac{5}{8}$ "
Ninth "	2 x $2\frac{1}{2}$ "	$2\frac{3}{8}$ x $2\frac{7}{8}$ "
Sixteenth "	$1\frac{3}{8}$ x $1\frac{5}{8}$ "	$1\frac{3}{4}$ x 2 "

[1] Fractional variations of plates were commonplace in early photography.

TABLE No. 2   A general chart of the standard plastic miniature case showing the measurement of mold variations. (Usually to the nearest ⅛ inch), the type of hinge and method of fastening hinges used by each of the major casemakers.

CASEMAKER — Manufacturer's trade name and Patent dates appearing on label	CASE SIZE (in inches)						HARDWARE & APPLICATION	
	Whole	*Half*	*Quarter*	*Sixth*	*Ninth*	*Sixteenth*	*Type Hinge*	Method of Fastening
Attributed, unmarked S. Peck & Co. CA 1852-1853	——	——	4½x5	3½x3⅞	——	——	Butt—U type	Molded in Plastic
S. Peck & Co. pat. 1854	——	5¼x6¼	4⅛x5	3½x3⅞	2⅝x3⅛	——	Butt—U type	Molded in Plastic, Metal Reinforced
Peck pat. 1854 Genuine union case Halvorson's 1855	——	——	4x4⅞	3⅜x3¾	2½x3	——	Butt—UL type	Smooth Head Face Riveted
Peck pat. 1854 Genuine union case Halvorson 1855 Peck pat. 1856	——	——	4¼x5	3½x3⅞	2½x3	——	Butt—UL type	Molded in Plastic, Metal Reinforced
S. Peck & Co. Manufacturers No pat. date	7 9/16 x 9 5/16	——	——	3⅜x3¾	2½x3	——	Butt—UL type	Smooth Head, Face Riveted
Scovill Mfg. Co. No pat. date	——	——	4x5	3⅜x3¾	2½x3	1⅞x2⅛	Butt—UL type	Smooth Head, Face Riveted
A. P. Critchlow & Co. Pat. 1856	——	——	4⅛x5	3½x3⅞	2½x3	——	Butt—UL type	Smooth Head, Face Riveted
A. P. Critchlow & Co. Pats. 1856-1857	——	5x6⅛	4x5	3⅜x3¾	2½x3	——	Butt—UL type	Smooth Head, Face Riveted
Littlefield, Parsons & Co. Pats. 1856-1857	7 3/16 x 9⅛	5x6¼	4x4⅞	3⅜x3¾	2½x3	1⅞x2⅛	Butt—UL type	Rosette Head Face Riveted
Florence Manufacturing Co. under L. P. & Co. pats.	——	4⅞x6⅛	——	——	——	——	Butt—UL type	Smooth Head Face Riveted
Holmes, Booth & Hayden No pat. date	——	——	——	3⅜x3¾	2½x3	1⅞x2⅛	Butt—UL type	Smooth Head Face Riveted
Wadhams Mfg. Co. Pat. 1858	——	——	——	——	2⅝x3⅛	1⅞x2⅛	Pivot-friction type	Molded in Plastic
F. Goll Attributed-unmarked	——	5x6¼	——	3⅜x3⅞*	——	——	Butt—UL type	Smooth Head Face Riveted

All plastic cases used a friction type clasp and were fastened in the same manner as the hinges.
NOTE: There is a possibility other sizes (represented by the blank spaces above) were made by the individual casemaker but were not available at time of printing.
* Rail riveted as well as face riveted.

Notes to the Text

CHAPTER 1

1. The term "Daguerreian Artist" was the name adopted by the pioneer photographers (Daguerreotypists) as an identification of their profession. Spelling varied with the individual operators; the most popular terms were *daguerreian, daguerrian,* and *daguerrean.*

2. Graham Reynolds, *English Portrait Minatures,* Adam and Charles Black, London, 1952, pp. 164–165.

3. After the introduction of the ambrotype in the 1850's the thickness of the miniature case increased to three-quarter inch and frequently to seven-eights of an inch.

4. A series of analytical experiments was conducted by the authors on a number of miniature cases (wood-frame). Paper and cloth as well as leather-covered cases were taken apart to determine quality of the materials used and methods of workmanship. The results of the tests will be found under notes 5, 6, 7, and 8. (*See also* Figs. 2, 3, and 4 for illustrations.)

5. Interestingly, earlier (1840's) cases have generally withstood the ravages of time better than the later, laminated ones. In many instances, the material covering the laminated wood covers has shown a tendency to crack at the tongue and groove joint. The warping and twisting of the cover was controlled and minimized by added thickness at the side rails in both methods of construction.

6. In a test made by the authors, a number of "tops" of leather were immersed in water until completely saturated. They were then removed and twisted (like a chamois) to take out the excess moisture. After being smoothed out and dried, the leather pieces (also paper and cloth) retained their original design and appearance except for a fractional stretching of the material caused by the twisting.

7. The authors found that, even after a hundred years, the glue used by some casemakers showed a remarkable resistance to being water soluble. Whether the glue originally used was designed to be "waterproof" is questionable. The glue generally used in casemaking was of amber color and cake-type. It was necessary to heat until melted before application.

8. From a standpoint of durability the greatest single failure in miniature case construction (including plastic cases) was that of the hinge arrangement. More than 2,000 cases examined by the authors showed that at least fifty percent had developed some weakness around the hinge construction.

9. This casemaking characteristic has proved helpful in identifying the product of a particular manfacturer. In addition to the sharp edge line, the casemaker also made decorative lines along the rails of case which varied as to spacing and number.

10. The exact color of a leather case in its original state is very hard to determine. The authors have concluded, through study, that the majority were medium brown or dark tan, however, black was also common. A few were painted a bright orange in the 1850's.

11. Sometimes a casemaker used a cut piece of newspaper or an old billhead for this purpose. Occasionally, a date may be found on these which may be helpful in establishing the time of manufacture.

12. Wholesale prices on brass mats in 1850 were: burnished, $62\frac{1}{2}$ cents a dozen, unburnished, 50 cents a dozen. Gold covered paper mats, plain and decorated, were occasionally used in place of the brass ones. Fancy paper mats sold for 50 cents to $4.00 a dozen in 1850.

13. H. H. Snelling, *Dictionary of the Photographic Art,* 1854. In the rear of this book is found Anthony's Catalog, pp. vii–viii (introduction).

14. On a wholesale level, one manufacturer's price for the leather-covered case in 1843 was $5.00 a dozen. B. Newhall, *The Daguerreotype in America,* 1961, p. 129.

By 1850, an imitation leather (paper) case, "sixth" size (*see* size Chart), was quoted at $1.50 a dozen, the "figured morrocco case at

$4.00 per dozen, and the plain at $3.50 a dozen. This 1850 quotation included the mat and glass. Another case quotation taken from L. Chapman's list in 1850 included the "sixth" size at $15.00 to $198.00 per gross. His price for cases inlaid with mother-of-pearl ranged from $90.00 to $1,152.00 per gross for the same size. *The Daguerreian Journal,* Vol. 1 (1850). Advertisements.

The selling price of the miniature case was often quoted by the daguerreian artists in their advertisements, but the price included the photograph. It is, therefore, impossible to pinpoint a retail price of the miniature case from this source.

CHAPTER 2

1. The first financing of Peck by Scovill Manufacturing Co. had been done by its New York store but after the co-partnership was formalized, the Scovill Co. increased its investment to $5,000. The "Hall property" had been secured as a factory site, and Peck was put in charge. Information, courtesy of Dr. P. W. Bishop from his notes on Scovill business papers.

2. *Ibid.*

3. Although the plastic composition used for daguerreotype cases was ordinarily colored black or shades of brown, other colors have been noted in rare instances. Katherine McClinton in her book, *A Handbook of Popular Antiques,* 1946, p. 229, notes that some small plastic cases with screw-on tops were made in red, green, and tan colored composition. The authors saw an orange plastic case of "sixth" size in one collection.

4. Peck's cases manufactured under his 1854 and 1856 patents and also the patent of Halvorson were reinforced on the inside part of the covers with a light piece of rectangular or, sometimes, oval cardboard. This practice was dropped in later cases bearing the name *S. Peck and Co., Manufacturers* (no patent references appeared on label, *see* Fig. 28).

5. The original letters from the United States Patent Office will be found in an envelope containing Samuel Peck's U. S. Letters Patent records (11,758) at the National Archives, Washington, D. C.

6. The authors are indebted to Mr. J. Harry Du Bois, engineering editor of *Plastics World,* for supplying information about Alfred P. Critchlow from his own research files.

7. The authors examined many cases bearing the patent label of A. P. Critchlow which were of varying shades of browns as well as black composition.

8. It is puzzling to the authors as to why the cases made by Samuel Peck (label showing patent by Peck, 1854 and label showing combined patents Peck, 1854, Halvorson, 1855, and Peck, 1856, *see* Figs. 21 and 23) used identical molded type hinges while the cases (label showing patent by Peck, 1854 and Halvorson, 1855, *see* Fig. 22) used an entirely different arrangement and were face riveted (*see* Appendix 1).

9. Many surviving cases show a tendency to warp, especially on the cover side, and to assume a concave shape. This condition was perhaps caused by the heat of an attic where they must have lain for many years—heat that probably exceeded 100 degrees Fahrenheit. The authors conducted an experiment to determine the degree of heat necessary to make the plastic composition pliable. The case in question, which had a concave warp, was stripped of its interior furnishings and placed in hot water (140–160 degrees) for one half-hour. In that length of time, the heat had penetrated the composition. After its removal from the water, the composition proved stiffly pliable, and by repeating this process several times, we were able to restore the case cover(s) almost to its original shape. We also found that most plastic cases can stand a brisk scrubbing with a soft toothbrush in lukewarm water using a mild liquid detergent and a thorough rinsing to remove surface dirt. However, we avoided such a cleaning process on some of the earlier cases that appear to water spot or stain easily.

10. Information, courtesy of Dr. P. W. Bishop, from his notes on Scovill business papers.

11. The partnership between Samuel Peck and Scovill Co. was an interesting one. Peck set his own prices allowing the Scovill purchasing agent ten percent and the freedom to buy elsewhere. Peck was independent of the Waterbury branch of Scovill Co. in that he made his own hinges and clasps. The Scovill Co. advanced two-thirds of the purchase price when cases were received and the balance on 90 day notes. The commission paid the New York store provided the wherewithal to obtain silks, velvets, and leather from England and France if Scovill's agents visited these markets. By the time the joint stock company was formed in 1855, Peck's cases were in wide demand in America and abroad. However, the New York store complained increasingly of delayed deliveries and faulty workmanship.

12. *Ibid.*

CHAPTER 3

1. Mr. Japhet Curtis, Jr. the sole manufacturer of the Stiles' Magnifying Case is listed in *The Daguerreian Journal,* Vol. 1, p. 12 (*see* Fig. 34) as being located in Southbury, Connecticut. However, a later advertisement for "Magnifying Cases" in *The Daguerreian Journal,* p. 220, gives Curtis' address as Southford, Connecticut.

2. An article on Mascher's stereoscope patent case appeared in the *Scientific American,* May 28, 1853.

3. Mascher was granted an improvement on his original stereoscope case patent, Feb. 19, 1856. The improvement consisted of binding together in the style of a book "any convenient number of suitable pictures (which may be interspersed with blank or printed leaves of paper or other substance) in combination with the 'supplementary lid, or adjustable flap' containing a lens or lenses attached to one of the lids of the said book."

Other stereoscope case patents were issued to J. Stull, Phila., Pa. (12,451) and W. Loyd, Phila., Pa. (14,670).

4. A picture of this medallion may be seen in *Humphrey's Journal,* Vol. VII (1855), p. 12.

5. *The Daguerreian Journal,* Vol. 1 (1850), p. 238.

6. *The Daguerreian Journal,* Vol. 111 (1851), p. 80.

7. *Ibid.*

8. Some papier mâché book-style cases (inlaid mother-of-pearl) were constructed to hold two portraits; they included a mid-section which could be moved like a page in a book.

9. Velvet cases are mostly found in rosy red shades, greens, and blues.

10. It would be difficult to pinpoint the exact date of the first albums. One of the early forerunners of the conventional album was Mascher's improvement on his stereoscope case (*see* notes Chapter 3, item 3). Scovill Manufacturing Co. carried an accordion type case arrangement that held six pictures. *Humphrey's Journal,* Vol. X (1858), p. 147.

11. According to Robert Taft's book, *Photography and the American Scene,* 1938, p. 143, albums were advertised to sell from $5.00 to $40.00. The authors have examined many albums of the 1860's and have found that an inexpensive paper-type was manufactured, which must have cost considerably less than $5.00—some undoubtedly but a few cents.

CHAPTER 4

1. The only comprehensive information the authors could find on the methods of cylinder die embossing was in a booklet titled *Embossing,* written by P. J. Lawler, Maulden, Mass., 1891. The Library of Congress has a copy.

2. F. W. Fairholt, *A Dictionary of Terms in Art,* 1854, p. 148.

3. A great many U. S. Design Patents were issued for carpet designs during the 1840's. Many of these were also designated for use with other materials, and some of the patterns resembled those seen on miniature case covers.

4. F. W. Fairholt's book in *A Dictionary of Terms in Art,* 1854, p. 36, writes of the wearing of Albs and other ecclesiastical vestments, "but in consequence of the revival of interest in all matters relating to Christian Art, they have lately been revived in a portion of the Romish Church."

5. *Humphrey's Journal,* Vol. IV (Dec. 1852), p. 269.

6. In addition to miniature cases being made especially for the deceased, three patents were issued for "tombstone monumentals." The following U. S. Patents are listed in order of dates: Solon Jenkins, Jr., West Cambridge, Mass., for "Securing Daguerreotypes in Monumental Stones," Mar. 11, 1851 (7,974); J. Bergstresser, Berrysburg, Pa. for "Monumental Daguerreotype Case" (this had an inner central frame and outer frame cast together on the same glass plate), Feb. 8, 1859 (22,850); H. S. Jones and S. S. Drake, Stoughton, Mass., Dec. 6, 1859 (26,370).

7. *The American Journal of Photography and the Allied Arts and Sciences,* Seeley and Garbanati, N. Y., Vol. 1 (1858), p. 94.

Notes on Plates

Plate 1. Rare. Highly prized by collectors. One of three known whole plate sizes. Copied from the famous American painting "The Landing of Columbus," by John Vanderlyn (1775–1852). The original now hangs in the Rotunda of the United States Capitol. Under the painting an inscription reads "At the Island of Guanahani, West Indies, Oct. 12, 1492."

Some confusion exists about the date of manufacture for cases of this design. Through the courtesy of Miss Josephine Cobb, the authors examined a case of this design for hinge arrangement and surface appearance. In our opinion it would date from 1857–1860. Katherine McClinton in her book, "Handbook of Popular Antiques" (1946) gives a patent date of Nov. 1, 1877. A search of United States Letters Patents and also Design Patents (1857–1880) as well as through copyright records with the help of the Library of Congress was not rewarding. Daguerreotype cases were not often used after 1870, possibly this type of picture case was revived for the great Centennial Exhibition at Philadelphia in 1876. The Scovill Manufacturing Co. dates the case somewhere between 1860–1880. The company is rumored to have paid the United States Mint $3,000 for casting the die.

Plate 2. Uncommon. Subject not identified.

Plate 3. Very rare. The title ascribed reflects the authors' interpretation of the subject matter. We may have overlooked literary or historical meaning.

Plate 4. Rare. Highly prized by collectors. One of three known whole plate sizes. Copied from, "Washington Crossing the Delaware," by Emanuel Leutze (1816–1868), who is best remembered for this historical painting.

Plate 5. Produced in quantity. All cases designed by Goll are highly prized by collectors. Copied from 1835 painting of the same name done by Asher B. Durand (1796–1886).

Plate 6. Rare. Highly prized by collectors. The die is said to have been copied after the work of the French sculptor Jean Antoine Houdon (1741–1828). He came to America with Benjamin Franklin in September 1785 to do a bust of Washington at Mt. Vernon.

Plate 7. Rare. Highly prized by collectors. Produced in quantity. A model for this monument was accepted in 1850 from American sculptor Thomas Crawford (1814–1857). The cornerstone was laid in that year, and the equestrian statue of Washington with smaller statues of Patrick Henry and Thomas Jefferson was unveiled Feb. 22, 1858. Other statues were added later including one of Chief-Justice John Marshall. Greatest height of monument is 60 feet, and the diameter of its base is 86 feet.

Plate 8. Rare. A variant with patriotic border. Very fine workmanship.

Plate 9. Very rare. Highly prized by collectors. Many designs for "A proposed Washington Monument" were submitted to the Congress and public in the mid-nineteenth century. Among them was one shown in a lithograph by Benjamin F. Smith Jr., in 1851. It was "Respectfully dedicated to the President and citizens of the United States" by the publishers Smith and Jenkins, N. Y. The case design illustrated here is almost identical to the Smith lithograph. Smith, an artist and a man of many talents, may have designed the die for this case.

Plate 10. Very rare. The scene probably depicts San Francisco Harbor.

Plate 11. Producd in quantity. A symbolic design of a strong America on land and sea.

Plates 12, 13. Uncommon. Fires in the era of the miniature case were very frequent, especially in the cities, and the dedicated volunteer became a symbolic figure on the American scene.

Plate 14. Produced in quantity. Symbolic of agriculture. A larger "one-quarter" size was also made.

Plate 15. Produced in quantity and in several variants. Highly prized by collectors. Copied from a Currier and Ives lithograph titled, "American Country Life; Summer's Evening." The original lithograph was engraved in 1855 by Fanny Palmer (1812–1876). The English-born Mrs. Palmer came to the United States in the early 1840's. A landscape artist, she was employed by the firm of Currier and Ives for many years.

Plate 16. Uncommon. Theme possibly from literature.

Plate 17. Extremely rare as are all scenes on leather-covered miniature cases. Washington Irving's residence, "Sunnyside," along the Hudson River, was once called "Wolfert's Roost."

Plate 18. Extremely rare. An unidentified scene. One of a series, of scenes with identical star borders. (See Plate 17).

Plate 19. Uncommon. The scene with the Gothic cottage in the background resembles the later twentieth century painting by Grant Wood, "American Gothic."

Plates 20, 21. Produced in quantity and in several variants. Symbolic of agriculture.

Plate 22. Uncommon. Probably represents life on the farm.

Plate 23. A rare case. The title "Going to Market" (inscribed on the die) might have been inspired from an old English rhyme published in 1844 in "The Nursery Rhymes of England."

> To market, to market, a gallop, a trot
> To bring some meat to put in the pot;
> Three pence a quarter, a groat a side,
> If it hadn't been killed it must have died.

Plate 24. Produced in quantity and in other variants. Collecting butterflies was a popular hobby in this era.

Plate 25. A rare case. The inspiration for this die undoubtedly came from the old English rhyme "Bobby Shafto." Sir Walter Scott in Redgauntlet referred to the rhyme as "an old Northumbrian ditty."

> Bobby Shafto's gone to sea,
> Silver buckles on his knee;
> He'll come back to marry me,
> Bonny Bobby Shafto!
>
> Bobby Shafto's fat and fair,
> Combing down his yellow hair;
> He's my love forevermore,
> Bonny Bobby Shafto!

Plate 26. Produced in quantity. Case also made in an octagon shape.

Plate 27. Uncommon.

Plate 28. Produced in quantity. The era of the miniature case witnessed an awakening interest in music.

Plate 29. Uncommon. In the authors' opinion the design portrays a Christmas scene.

Plate 30. Produced in quantity. A popular sentimental design.

Plate 31. A rare case.

Plate 32. Very rare. The lyre, artist's palette, and books symbolize the arts.

Plate 33. Extremely rare. A well executed design in leather.

Plate 34. Very rare. Horse racing was the most popular sport in America in this era.

Plate 35. Produced in quantity. Highly prized by collectors. Theme from mythology.

Plate 36. Uncommon. A later variant of "Cupid and the Wounded Stag." The die casting is not as clearly and sharply defined as the earlier version, (see Plate 35).

Plate 37. Rare. Probably inspired by the biblical story of the finding of Moses by two Egyptian women.

Plate 38. Uncommon. It is possible that this is the same case referred to in Katherine McClinton's "Handbook of Popular Antiques" (1946) as Pope Leo by diemaker J. Smith.

Plate 39. Probably not made in quantity because of its small size.

Plate 40. Produced in quantity. Highly prized by collectors. Said to have been copied from a painting, "The Faithful Hound," by Johann Gellert. The Frick Art Reference Library, New York City, at the author's request, searched its files and found no record of such a painting. However, there was a listing for a Johann Gellert (born in Prague, Czechoslovakia, 1821), a landscape painter.

Plate 41. Uncommon. One of the few cases depicting a subtle theme.

Plate 42. Produced in quantity. Highly prized by collectors. An early case. Copied from the painting, "The Calmady Children," by Sir Thomas Lawrence. The daughters of C. B. Calmady were painted in 1824. Emily was born in 1818 and Laura Anne was born in 1820. The Metropolitan Museum of Art owns the original painting.

Plate 43. Produced in quantity by A. P. Critchlow and also his successors Littlefield, Parsons & Co. Highly prized by collectors. Design based on a silver piece which was exhibited at the New York Crystal Palace in 1853 by J. Angell of London, the literary figure of Sir Roger de Coverly. The scene was considered the best of the opening group of sketches by Joseph Addison (1672-1719) and Richard Steele (1672-1729) in their publication "Spectator," circa 1711.

Plate 44. Uncommon. The falcon was a favorite European hunting bird. A domestic falcon often graced the Renaissance pageants and court scenes.

Plate 45. Rare. The Scotsman shown may be Rob Roy (1671-1734), famed Highland outlaw, who figured in the novel by Sir Walter Scott.

Plate 46. Rare. The inscription "Havelock" identifies the military figure as Sir Henry Havelock (1795-1857). During his career in the

British army, General Havelock was one of the heroes of the Indian Mutiny.

Plate 47. Uncommon.

Plate 48. One of the first plastic cases produced by Peck. Probably made in some quantity. Rare. On the outer circle, above the open Bible is inscribed "Our Father who art in Heaven." A reference Matthew VI: 9, appears just below. This unsigned design forms the rear cover of the "Memorial" (see Plate 62), which was signed by R. Paine.

Plate 49. Very rare. From early times, angels have been used in artistic iconography to symbolize a divine mission. Possibly the angel Gabriel.

Plates 50, 51. Rare. Symbolic compositions. Infant mortality was high during the miniature case era.

Plate 52. Rare. Simplicity and precision were used by the unknown die engraver to simulate a leaded glass window in the shape of a cross.

Plates 53. 54. Produced in very large quantity. Two of the most popular cross designs made during the Civil War.

Plate 55. Uncommon. Cross designs were created by the medieval designer in an almost endless variety and were used both as ornaments and symbols. Many of Frederick Key's designs were built around the central theme of the cross. His art in this field is unsurpassed.

Plate 56. Uncommon.

Plate 57. Produced in quantity. A design similar to those used in English heraldry.

Plate 58. Rare. The flowers surrounding the Cross are finely done in very deep relief.

Plate 59. Rare. A design using symbols of the Church.

Plate 60. Only case of this design known. The theme is symbolic of death and a voyage to the next world. The spade and pall represent death. The radiating lines beyond the ship indicate the light of another world.

Plate 61. Uncommon. The workmanship of the central flower theme is finely executed in detail. A double "sixth size" case.

Plate 62. Rare. One of the earliest cases made of plastic composition. The only design die signed by R. Paine. Samuel Peck ordered this die from "Paine of Springfield," which cost $105.00—an amount Peck thought "rather mighty" at a time when his orders were not to exceed $60.00. Another almost identical variant was made later but did not bear Paine's signature.

Plate 63. One of the popular large size cases in the 1850 decade.

Plate 64. Uncommon. Probably a funerary urn.

Plate 65. Rare.

Plates 66-68. Produced in quantity. Three examples of inexpensive miniature cases made during the Civil War. All patriotic cases found to date reflect the North's sentiments and slogans. Patriotic cases may have been made in the South, but none have been found to date.

Plate 69. Produced in quantity. A very popular theme in the era before the Civil War.

Plate 70. Produced in quantity. Highly prized by collectors.

Plates 71, 72. Plate 71 is more uncommon than 72. The design reflects the Union's pride in the "Monitor." It is the authors' opinion that a different die-engraver was used for each version.

Plates 73, 74. Two rare designs illustrating the Union navy at war.

Plates 75-77. Uncommon. Variants.

Plate 78. Uncommon. A variant of the crossed cannon design found in Fig. 30 (text illustrations).

Plate 79. Rare. Represents camp life in the Union army.

Plate 80. Uncommon.

Plate 81. A rare case. Animal designs were seldom used on the leather-covered case.

Plate 82. Uncommon. The stag frequently symbolized solitude and purity of life.

Plate 83. Rare. The swan is a symbol in poetry of remote unworldly beauty.

Plate 84. Uncommon. A sentimental pictorial theme.

Plate 85. Uncommon. Domestic birds and bird cages were often pictured in the ladies' monthly magazines of the era.

Plate 86. Produced in quantity. The popularity of sketches by John J. Audubon created a demand for bird themes in other fields of art.

Plate 87. Produced in some quantity.

Plate 88. Rare. An unusual woody vine border.

Plates 89, 90. Produced in quantity.

Plates 91-93. Produced in quantity. The vase of flowers and bird theme had been widely used in decoration and illustration for at least two centuries before 1850.

Plates 94, 95. Produced in quantity. Unusual abstract designs.

Plate 96. Produced in quantity. Highly prized by collectors. A composition symbolic of eternal conflict.

Plate 97. Uncommon. A distinctive design suggestive of Egypt.

Plate 98. Uncommon. Probably taken from a North American Indian mythological tale of the "Deluge." The bird symbolizes the good being destroying the snake which caused the earth to become flooded.

Plate 99. Uncommon. A simple, effective, fruit design.

Plate 100. Produced in some quantity. The grape more than any other fruit was widely used in case designs. A biblical symbol of peace and abundance.

Plate 101. Uncommon.

Plate 102. Produced in quantity.

Plate 103. Rare. Possibly a religious theme.

Plate 104. Uncommon. In Christian art, the cherry is symbolic of sweetness of character derived from good works.

Plates 105, 106. Uncommon.

Plate 107. Rather rare.

Plate 108. Widely produced in "half" and "quarter" sizes.

Plate 109. Rare. Similar tiny fruit baskets were sometimes used on the border designs of large cases.

Plate 110. Extremely rare. Photographic reproductions of the case as well as the label are on display at the Pro-Phy-Lac-Tic Brush Co. plant at Florence, Mass.

Plate 111. Rare.

Plate 112. Produced in very large quantity. In poetry, the lily has always shared honors with the rose and violet.

Plate 113. Produced in quantity. One of the many variants of the "two lily" case. The authors have counted eleven variants to date.

Plate 114. Produced in moderate quantity.

Plate 115. Uncommon.

Plate 116. Uncommon. A motif used in America by the Pennsylvania Dutch.

Plate 117. Uncommon. Symbolic of farewell and departure.

Plate 118. Produced in limited quantity.

Plate 119. Produced in quantity. The thistle is the national emblem and symbol of Scotland.

Plate 120. Uncommon. Probably represents one of the wood nymphs of mythology.

Plate 121. Rare. At one time the golden rose was considered so honorable a present that none but crowned heads were thought worthy to give or receive it.

Plate 122. Uncommon. Since ancient times, the rose has been a symbol of love, beauty, and courage.

Plates 123-126. Generally produced in large quantity. Some variants are rare. A group of flower designs often called "The Delicate Rose Case." There were at least thirty similar designs patterned after the simple design shown in Plate 123. An interesting theory concerning these cases was that the number of leaves on the lower branches often denoted the date of the case; thus, if the number of leaves on the lower branch showed four and the leaves on the other lower branch showed five, the date of the case would be 1845. However, a factual study of the cases manufactured by Wm. Shew and also those made by Gordon and Studley disproves this theory by establishing that the known date of their specific business address did not coincide with the conjectured date of manufacture. The case shown in Plate 124 was sold in 1845. Some variations of this design show a five and six combination of leaves, while others show a five and seven (*see* Plate 126). Sometime in the early 1840's the first of these designs was produced, and it proved increasingly popular as the decade progressed. During the height of their popularity 1845-1848, many casemakers were busy manufacturing variations of this general pattern. Pretlove (die-engraver) made at least two rose designs—a two-rose leafy border (Plate 123) and a four-rose scroll border. The Shew brothers made at least three variations almost identical to Plates 123, 124, and 125.

Plate 127. Produced in quantity.

Plate 128. Produced in limited quantity. One of the "medallion series" case. Borders are identical, motif varies with subject. See Plate 102. As a set these should be highly prized by collectors.

Plate 129. Produced in large quantity.

Plate 130. Rare.

Plate 131. One of the most popular case designs in the early 1850's. Variants were made by a number of casemakers.

Plate 132. Rare.

Plate 133. Uncommon. One of Pretlove's finest designs.

Plate 134. Produced in quantity. Design copied for one of the first transitional covers produced in plastic.

Plate 135. Produced in quantity. Another "series" case. The border remains identical while the motif changes.

Plate 136. Produced in quantity.

Plate 137. Produced in limited quantity. A "series" case, the outer border remains identical (*see* Plate 211), while the master motif has many variants.

Plate 138. Uncommon. The valentine often used the floral, bow-knot design in the first half of the nineteenth century.

Plate 139. Produced in limited quantity. Inlaid mother-of-pearl papier-mâché cases are highly prized by collectors.

Plate 140. Rare. Probably the most striking design of the early cases. It is the authors' opinion, based on careful study, that the first cases with this design were made in 1841. A similar design, not illustrated, was also made in about the same period.

Plate 141. Produced in large quantity and a number of variants.

Plate 142. Very rare.

Plate 143. Uncommon.

Plate 144. Uncommon.

Plate 145. Uncommon.

Plate 146. Very rare. Few cases were produced with silk as a covering material. The die-engraver's name is below the design in reverse, and properly reads—A. C. Paquet . . . Philada.

Plate 147. Uncommon.

Plate 148. Produced in some quantity. This border design was used with a number of other varying motifs. A similar case was made by a competing casemaker.

Plate 149. Produced in quantity.

Plate 150. Uncommon. An unusual border for a tiny case.

Plate 151. Rare.

Plate 152. Uncommon. The acorn leaf design was widely used in pottery decoration.

Plate 153. Uncommon.

Plate 154. Produced in some quantity.

Plate 155. Uncommon.

Plate 156. Uncommon. A distinctive case because of its fine quality pigskin covering.

Plate 157. Uncommon.

Plate 158. Produced in some quantity.

Plate 159. Uncommon.

Plate 160. Rare.

Plate 161. Rare.

Plate 162. Uncommon. Suggestive of Gothic architecture.

Plate 163. Produced in quantity. In Greek mythology a nymph Amalthea was said to have possessed a miraculous goat's horn given her by Zeus. The cornucopia—symbol of plenty—was often represented in works of art, especially in the Roman period.

Plate 164. Uncommon.

Plate 165. Uncommon. Similar designs found in Egyptian tombs.

Plate 166. Produced in moderate quantity.

Plate 167. Produced in quantity. A symbolic composition.

Plate 168. Uncommon. The origin of the design probably dates to the knight's girdle, popular in fourteenth century England.

Plate 169. Rare. Possibly the origin of the chain and buckle design dates back to James IV of Scotland and the legend of the iron belt.

Plate 170. Produced in some quantity. Derived from heraldry.

Plate 171. Uncommon. The scallop shell was the emblem of St. James the Great and became an insignia of the pilgrims returning from the Holy Land.

Plate 172. Produced in some quantity.

Plate 173. Uncommon.

Plate 174. Rare. Highly prized by collectors. A token of remembrance.

Plate 175. Produced in some quantity. A prize cup similar to those awarded in the 1850's.

Plate 176. Rare. Probably depicting the popular Swedish opera star Jenny Lind.

Plate 177. Uncommon.

Plate 178. Uncommon.

Plate 179. Uncommon.

Plate 180. Uncommon.

Plate 181. Uncommon.

Plate 182. Uncommon. The scroll was a decorative ornament used from the earliest period.

Plates 183, 184. Produced in some quantity.

Plate 185. Produced in some quantity from 1846-1850. The acanthus leaf scroll was widely used in the decorative arts. A plant used in Greek and Italian garden plots because of its beautiful leaves.

Plate 186. Produced in some quantity.

Plate 187. Uncommon.

Plate 188. Uncommon.

Plate 189. Produced in quantity.

Plate 190. Very rare. The Lord's Prayer central motiff (see Plate 48) has been changed to an engraved metal disk. Embellishment has been added to the die.

Plate 191. Uncommon.

Plate 192. Uncommon.

Plate 193. Rare. All the distinctive characteristics of the Brady case (see Fig. 13) are evident in this example. The authors believe that this case was made by Brady or an associate.

Plate 194. Rare. One of Peck's early designs.

Plate 195. Uncommon. Inside the center motif a man's head may be seen.

Plate 196. Produced in large quantity in both cloth and paper. Variations were also popular and numerous.

Plate 197. Uncommon. A nicely done case in cardboard.

Plate 198. Uncommon.

Plate 199. Uncommon. A case design used on both cover and bottom. Later cases sometimes used this design only on the bottom part of the case.

Plate 200. Uncommon. J. Smith, more than any other known die-designer, used geometric patterns and themes for his creations.

Plate 201. Produced in quantity. The case illustrated was exported to Ireland, sold by an Irish photographer, and returned to America by an Irish immigrant.

Plate 202. Very rare. The photograph inside the case bears the date 1859.

Plate 203. Uncommon. As a manufacturer Holmes, Booth, and Hayden sometimes placed a wholesaler's trade label in the rear of their cases. An identical type case to plate 203 was found with the name of Willard and Co. (see Fig. 32) on the inside cover replacing the usual Holmes, Booth and Hayden label.

Plate 204. Uncommon design when used as both cover and bottom. This design was often used as a bottom cover when the top cover design was elaborate.

Plate 205. Produced in quantity.

Plate 206. Uncommon.

Plate 207. Rare.

Plate 208. Uncommon. One of the few F. Key designs that did not have a religious theme.

Plate 209. Uncommon.

Plate 210. Produced in limited quantity.

Plate 211. Produced in some quantity. One of a series having the same border and a changing motif.

Plate 212. Rare. One of F. Key's finest designs.

Plate 213. Uncommon.

Plate 214. Produced in quantity during the Civil War.

Plate 215. Uncommon.

Plate 216. Rather rare.

Plates 217, 218. Produced in quantity.

Plate 219. One of the most popular cases produced during the 1840's. There are five or more variants of this design, all produced in some quantity.

Plates 220, 221. Uncommon.

Plate 222. Very rare. An optical illusion—one of the most unusual designs produced for the miniature case industry. The authors were amazed at sharpness of the design and precise workmanship of this case, which creates an illusion of movement by the cubes.

Plate 223. Uncommon. An optical illusion creating an effect of design intensification within the center of the circle.

Plate 224. Produced in some quantity. An optical illusion which has the effect of producing depth within the circle.

Plate 225. Produced in some quantity. Probably one of the first designs on cardboard for the miniature case industry.

Plate 226. Rather rare. Unusual design.

Plate 227. Produced in limited quantity. Gold tooled on fine leather.

Plate 228. Uncommon.

Plate 229. Uncommon.

Other Known Case Designs

A partial list of known cases, which are not illustrated in this book, appears on the following pages.

Over the years, many collectors have given a variety of names to an identical case. Frequently designs which are factually identified are often incorrectly titled by collectors. For example: *The Gypsy Fortune Teller,* Pl. 43 is often called "Washington's farewell to his mother." The nomenclature used in the following list of cases was frequently provided by case collectors.

Hundreds of designs in leather defy cataloguing because there exist no pictures of them. Many of the leather, paper, and cardboard cases have similar themes; because they differ only minutely in detail, they are not true variations but rather the outpourings of an art craft in a competitive market. And many variations share an almost identical central subject but differ somewhat in border design—this is evidenced in both the wood-frame coverings and those of plastic composition.

Measurements for sizes listed can be found in the Appendix. Casemakers, using the same die for the central theme, often produced larger or smaller cases by changing the border arrangement. The size of a particular case noted does not imply that other cases, larger or smaller, of the identical design have not been made. The known sizes have been noted by the authors.

An asterisk preceding case descriptions on the following list denotes that they were originally listed in Katherine McClinton's book *Handbook of Popular Antiques,* Random House, 1946. Occasionally, we have added informative data to Katherine McClinton's original entries.

THE HISTORY AND SENTIMENTS OF A PEOPLE

Historical American Scenes and Portraits

*1. Head of George Washington; leather; size unknown; maker unknown.
2. General Marion's sharing yams with British officer (from painting by John B. White); plastic, Littlefield, Parsons & Co.; octagan shape; "one-quarter" size.
*3. *Benedict Arnold's Escape; Charter Oak;* plastic; Wadham's Manufacturing Co.; size unknown.

Scenes of an Awakening America

4. Hunter and fallen deer; plastic; Littlefield, Parsons & Co.; "sixth" size.
*5. Country home scene; man, woman and boy near brook; plastic; Wadham's Manufacturing Co.; size unknown.
*6. An Elopement; plastic; Wadham's Manufacturing Co.; size unknown.
*7. Marriage of John Alden and Priscilla (from poem by Henry W. Longfellow); plastic; Littlefield, Parsons & Co.; size unknown.
*8. *Maude Muller* with hay fork (from poem of same name by John G. Whittier); plastic; Samuel Peck and Co.; size unknown.
*9. Beehive; leather (?); size unknown.
10. *The Tight Cork;* name inscribed in die; plastic; Samuel Peck and Co.; "sixth" size.
*11. *Odd Fellows* (fraternal); plastic; attributed Samuel Peck and Co.; size unknown.
12. Masonic (fraternal); plastic; attributed Samuel Peck and Co., size unknown.

Childhood Reflections

*13. Chasing butterflies; plastic; A. P. Critchlow & Co.; size unknown.
*14. Children with butterfly net, deer and cupids; plastic; Littlefield, Parsons & Co.; size unknown.
*15. Boy by a haystack with rabbit; plastic; Scovill Manufacturing Co.; size unknown.
*16. Children with lambs; plastic; maker unknown, F. Seiler, die-maker; size unknown.
17. Two children, one leaning on stile, the other holding rope with lamb; plastic; Littlefield, Parsons & Co.; oval shape; "one-sixteenth" size.
*18. Red Riding Hood (*Grimms' Fairy Tales*); plastic; Littlefield, Parsons & Co.; size unknown.
*19. Paul and Virginia (literary, story from Bernardin de St. Pierre (1788); plastic; Littlefield, Parsons & Co.; size unknown.

Pleasant Pastimes

*20. Pacing horse; plastic, Scovill Manufacturing Co.; 6½" x 3" size.
*21. Yacht design; plastic; Scovill Manufacturing Co.; 8½" x 5¾" size.

Art and Reflections From Abroad

*22. Cleopatra; plastic; Littlefield, Parsons & Co.; size unknown.
*23. Head of Julius Caesar; shell and scroll border; plastic; maker unknown; size unknown.
*24. Voyage of Cytherea (mythology); plastic; Samuel Peck and Co.; size unknown.
*25. Europa and the Bull (mythology); plastic; maker unknown; size unknown.
*26. Pope Pius, plastic, Samuel Peck and Co.; size unknown.
27. British Colonial soldier holding sword; plastic; Scovill Manufacturing Co.; "sixth" size.
*28. Lady Diana Mannering (literary); plastic; Littlefield, Parsons & Co.; size unknown.
*29. Fairy Head in Rose; plastic; Samuel Peck and Co.; size unknown.
*30. *Una* (from Spenser's *The Faerie Queene*); plastic; Wadham's Manufacturing Co.; size unknown.
31. Cameo of Shakespeare; plastic; maker unknown; F. Key, die-maker; size unknown.
*32. The Young Pretender; plastic; Holmes, Booth & Hayden; size unknown.
33. Two knights in battle, one fallen; leather; maker unknown; "sixth" size, *circa* 1841.

Religion and Death

*34. Church Window; plastic; Samuel Peck and Co.; size unknown.
35. Star and Cross; plastic; maker unknown; size unknown.

*36. Rebecca at the Well; plastic; Samuel Peck and Co.; size unknown.
*37. *The Vision of Ezekiel* (inscribed in die); plastic; Holmes, Booth & Hayden; size unknown.
38. Cross Formée with oval border motif; plastic; maker unknown; "one-ninth" size.
39. Toulouse cross, with curved diamond inside, cross motif, flower border; plastic; maker unknown; "sixth" size.

Outpourings of Patriotism

*40. Boy with flag and gun; plastic; Littlefield, Parsons & Co.; size unknown.
41. Shield surrounded by a star composed of small stars, "Union" on ribbon; plastic; attributed Littlefield, Parsons & Co.; "one-sixteenth" size.
42. Variation of Union and Constitution, eagle added above shield; plastic; attributed Littlefield, Parsons & Co.; "sixth" size.

NATURE THEMES

Birds and Beasts

43. Birds on fountain, basket-weave urn; plastic; attributed Samuel Peck and Co.; "sixth" size.
44. Two birds in fountain on pedestal; plastic; Littlefield, Parsons & Co.; "sixth" size. Same as leather-covered case (*see* Plate 80).
45. Kissing birds surrounded by leaf and two roses; plastic; maker unknown; oval shape; "one-sixteenth" size.

Fruit Designs

*46. Grapes; plastic; Holmes, Booth & Hayden; size unknown.

Fruit Arrangements

47. Vase of fruit; plastic; Holmes, Booth & Hayden; size unknown.

Mixed Flowers

48. Bunch of mixed flowers; plastic; Samuel Peck and Co.; size unknown.

Flower Arrangements in Vases and Urns

49. Urn of flowers suspended by chains; plastic; Littlefield, Parsons & Co.; "one-quarter" size.
*50. Basket of flowers (large); plastic; Littlefield, Parsons & Co.; size unknown.

Miscellaneous Flower and Leaf Motifs

51. Pressed flower motif; plastic; Littlefield, Parsons & Co.; size unknown.
52. Acorns on branch; plastic; maker unknown; "one-ninth" size.

TRADITIONAL AND GEOMETRIC DESIGNS

Conventional Art Motifs

53. Conch shell in oval center; heavy scroll border; plastic; Littlefield, Parsons & Co.; "sixth" size.

Gem Designs

54. Cameo head motif (eighteenth century French female); ornate border; plastic; attributed Littlefield, Parsons & Co.; "sixth" size.
55. Pearl motif; plastic; maker unknown, "one-ninth" size.

Oval Designs

56. Oval with basket-weave motif, tendril leaf border; plastic; attributed Samuel Peck and Co.; "one-quarter" size; F. Key, die-maker.
57. Raised gold oval with fleur de lis border motif; plastic; Littlefield, Parsons & Co.; octagon shape; "sixth" size.

Quatrefoil Motifs

58. Eight point star in center of quatrefoil, large leaf border; maker unknown; plastic; "one-ninth" size.

Miscellaneous Conventional Designs

59. Five point star center with four point strawberry border; plastic; maker unknown; octagon shape; "sixth" size.
*60. Geometric design, center painted gold; plastic; Samuel Peck and Co.; size unknown.
*61. Geometric design, center painted gold; plastic; Littlefield, Parsons & Co.; size unknown.
62. Six scallops center motif; plastic; Holmes, Booth & Hayden; "sixth" size.

Key to Abbreviations

Standard abbreviation, when used, is as listed in Webster's *New World Dictionary, College Edition*, and is used throughout. In addition, the following list of often repeated sources of research is shown below:

BD—Business directory or register for the city and date noted.

CD—City directory.

CSP—*The Citizens and Strangers Pictorial and Business Directory*, N. Y. C.

DJ—*The Daguerreian Journal.*

HJ—*Humphrey's Journal.*

MM—*Mercantile and Manufacturers Business Directory*, N.Y.C.; Phila.

NE—*New England Business Directory.*

NYA—*New York Advertising Business Directory.*

NYC—New York City.

NYHS—George C. Groce and David H. Wallace, *The New York Historical Society's Dictionary of Artists in America, 1564-1860.*

OPW—*O'Brien's Phila. Wholesale Business Directory.*

RC—Rinhart Collection.

RT—Robert Taft, *Photography and the American Scene.*

SBD—State Business Directory.

Biographies of Case Manufacturers

ANTHONY, EDWARD T. Pioneer daguerreian, manufacturer and jobber of photographic materials. Born NYC, 1818; died NYC, 1888. Studied civil engineering at Columbia College, NYC; graduated 1838 and afterwards worked on the Croton aqueduct NYC. Took lessons in daguerreotyping from Samuel Morse; photographer 1840-43 with United States Government Survey of Northeast Boundary conducted by Professor James Renwick. Proprietor of *National Daguerreotype Miniature Gallery* (Anthony, Edwards and Chilton), NYC, 1843; Anthony, Edwards and Co., 1844-45; Anthony, Clark and Co., 1846-47. Worked seasonally in Washington, D.C. from about 1843-47. Took photographs on April 12, 1844 of President John Tyler and on the same day one of John Quincy Adams. Merchant in photographic supplies in NYC from 1847; opened store at 205 Broadway, NYC, May 1, 1848. Importer of engravings, 1848; listed at same address until 1851. Became the leading dealer of photographic supplies in NYC during the 1850 decade. Listed at 308 Broadway, NYC, 1852-59; and at 501 Broadway, NYC, 1860. Partnership with brother Henry T. Anthony, NYC, 1852. In 1902 the E. and H. T. Anthony and Co. merged with the Scovill Manufacturing Co., Waterbury, Conn. The company again changed from Anthony and Scovill to Ansco in 1907 (*see* Scovill Manufacturing Co.).
Notes, courtesy of Dr. P. W. Bishop; research material, courtesy of Miss Josephine Cobb; DJ; CD, NYC; BD, NYC; RT; "The History of Ansco (courtesy of Ansco Co., Binghamton, N.Y.).

ANTHONY, HENRY T. Inventor, manufacturer of photographic supplies. Born . . . .; died NYC, 1884. Partnership with brother Edward T. Anthony from 1852. In charge of the manufacturing division of E. and H. T. Anthony and Co. Jan.

31, 1854, issued U. S. Patent (10,465) for *Press for Making Miniature Cases;* was issued (with Frank Phoebus, NYC) U. S. Patent (10,953) for *Apparatus for the Manufacture of Daguerreotype Cases,* May 23, 1854.
"History of Ansco" (courtesy of Ansco Co.); RT; U. S. Patent records.

BARN AND RANFLTE. Morocco case manufacturer. Listed at 60 Nassau St., NYC, 1856-57.
MM

BARNETT, F. Morocco case manufacturer. Listed at 129 William St., NYC, 1856-57.
MM

BARNET, JOHN. Manufacturer of jewel, miniature, surgical cases and daguerreotype cases at wholesale. Listed at 129 William St., NYC, 1856-57; at 91 Fulton St., NYC, 1859-60.
MM; SBD

BRADY, MATHEW B. Pioneer daguerreian; artist; surgical, jewel, and miniature casemaker; Civil War photographer. Born Warren County, N. Y., 1823 (?); died NYC, 1896. As young man copied sketches for artist William Page in upstate N.Y., and moved to NYC with Page in about 1837. Studied daguerreotyping 1840-42. Manufactured miniature cases 1843-45 (?). Opened first daguerreian gallery at 207 Broadway, NYC, 1844 (?). Listed as jewel, miniature and surgical case manufacturer at 187 Broadway (entrance 162 Fulton St.) NYC, 1844-46. Although listed as casemaker in *Doggett's Directory* for 1846, it is unlikely that Brady continued to make cases, for by this date he was already famous as a daguerreian artist. Published *Gallery of Illustrious Americans* in partnership with Francis D'Avignon and C. Edward Lester, 1850. Exhibited daguerreotypes in 1851 at Crystal Palace, London; won prize medal. Operated gallery in Washington, D. C. briefly in 1849, and later the Brady National Photographic Gallery from 1858 until Nov., 1881. Most famous for his Civil War battlefield photographs.

Josephine Cobb, "Mathew B. Brady's Photographic Gallery in Washington" 1955; CD; BD; James D. Horan, "Mathew Brady" 1955; Marcus Root, "The Camera and the Pencil," 1864; RT.

CHAPMAN, A. B.   Manufacturer of the "Union Composition Case." Location unknown, probably New York City.

Information courtesy of Time-Out Antiques, NYC.

CHAPMAN, LEVI L.   Jobber and manufacturer of photographic materials and daguerreotype cases, inventor. Listed at 81 William St., N.Y.C., as pocketbooks, 1840-42; listed Magic Strop, 102 William St., N.Y.C., 1843-45. Sold leather goods in 1846. Listed as jobber and manufacturer at 102 William St., N.Y.C., 1850-51. Had traveling agents to sell daguerreian materials which included cases, mats, preservers, daguerreotype plates, 1851-52 and later (?). Invented "improved photographic plate vise" in 1856 (*see* Fig. 14, Plate 184).

CD; "Scientific American," 1846; DJ; HJ.

CHEMIDLEN, NICOLAS   Maker of daguerreotype frames. Listed at 89 Reade St., N.Y.C., 1846.

CD

CHRISTY, Wm. M.   Manufacturer of Morocco cases. Listed at 82 Chestnut St., Phila., 1848.

OPW

CLARKE, J.   Manufacturer of Morocco cases. Listed at 29 Ferry St., N.Y.C., 1853.

CSP

COOPER, G.   Manufacturer of miniature cases and gold pen boxes, 1858.

NYA

CRITCHLOW, ALFRED P.   Horn button maker, die-sinker, pioneer plastic daguerreotype case manufacturer, inventor. Born Birmingham, England; died (?). Came to America and settled in Haydenville, Mass., 1843. Began the manufacture of horn buttons; moved after two or three years to Florence, Mass. Experimented with a plastic composition, later known as the Florence Compound; began the manufacture of plastic daguerreotype cases in 1853. Listed at Northampton, Mass., 1856 as A. P. Critchlow and Company. Was issued U. S. Patent (15,915) on Oct. 14, 1856 (reissue April 21, 1857) for "embracing riveted hinges." Plastic

daguerreotype cases carried his patent label. Sold business in 1857 and firm became known as Littlefield, Parsons & Co. Critchlow is believed to have later gone into the manufacture of tooth and hand brushes.

Information courtesy of J. Harry Du Bois; U. S. Patent records; NE, 1856.

De FOREST, BROS. & CO.   Miniature case manufacturer. Listed at (Benmingham) Derby, Conn., 1856-57.

NE

EATON, L & G   Miniature case manufacturer, Watertown, Conn., 1849.

NE

EICHMEYER, H. A.   Miniature case manufacturer, daguerreian, and inventor. Listed as casemaker (for all kinds of daguerreotype cases) at 46½ Walnut St., Phila., 1848. Listed as daguerreian at 62 Walnut St., Phila., 1854-55. Was issued Design Patent (694) on Feb. 27, 1855 for a miniature case.

OPW, 1848; SBD, 1854; U. S. Patent records.

FLORENCE MANUFACTURING CO.   Manufacturer of plastic daguerreotype cases, brushes, and other items of plastic composition. Corporation was formed May 23, 1866; organized by George A. Burr, Isaac S. Parsons and David G. Littlefield. Manufactured daguerreotype cases under Littlefield, Parsons & Co. patent. Name changed to Pro-Phy-Lac-Tic Brush Co. in the early 1920's and became a subsidiary of the Standard Oil Company (Ohio).

Information courtesy of Pro-Phy-Lac-Tic Brush Company; Collection of Mrs. Janie Wright (case).

FOULLEY, A.   Manufacturer of passe-partouts for daguerreotypes and photographs. Listed at 337 Broadway, N.Y.C., 1858.

NYA

GENNERT BROS.   Manufacturer of mattings and preservers, jobber. Listed at 106 Center St., N.Y.C., 1858-59.

NYA, 1858; SBD, 1859.

GOLL, FREDERICK P.   (*see* Die-engravers)

GORDON   (*see* Studley & Gordon)

GORDON, E.   Dealer and manufacturer of photographic apparatus and miniature cases. Listed at Elm St., corner White, N.Y.C., 1858-59. Listed in advertisement at 172 Center St., N.Y.C., 1860; advertisement locates establishment on line of railroad, case work done on fifth floor and store for photographic materials on ground floor.

NYA; SBD, 1859: Advertisement, "The American Journal of Photography," V. 3, p. 364.

GORDON AND WILLIS (*see* Simons and Willis) Morocco case manufacturer. Listed at 17 South 5 St., upstairs above Chestnut, Phila., 1848.
OPW

HALL, N. C. & CO. (Newell C. Hall) Daguerreotype case manufacturer. Listed at 12 Park, New Haven, Conn., 1856-57.
CD

HALL, OGDEN Miniature casemaker. Supplied daguerreotype cases for Scovill Manufacturing Co., from May, 1847 until 1850 (?). Listed at West Chapel, New Haven, Conn. 1848-50. Was in close relationship with Samuel Peck (casemaker, New Haven) until an "exchange of houses" in 1853. Listed at 38 West Chapel, New Haven, Conn., 1853-54. Not listed after 1853 in New Haven. Believed to have worked later for a casemaker in Oxford, Conn.
Notes, courtesy of Dr. P. W. Bishop; CD

HARNETT, J. F. Morocco case manufacturer. Listed at 13 John St., N.Y.C., 1856-57.
MM

HART AND WOODRUFF Daguerreotype case manufacturers. Listed Southampton, Conn., 1849.
NE

HENNING AND EYMANN (*see* Die-engravers) Daguerreotype casemakers (plastic); diesinkers and engravers. Active N.Y.C., 1859-60.

HILL, WALTER S. Brooklyn (N.Y.) daguerreotype frame maker, No. 9 Platt; res., 73 Hicks.

HOLMES, BOOTH & HAYDEN Brass manufacturers, and photographic materials. Manufactured plastic daguerreotype cases C. 1857 and later. Members of the firm were: John C. Booth, Israel Holmes, Henry Hayden. Listed at 37 Maiden Lane, N.Y.C., (home, Waterbury, Conn.) 1854-58. Henry Hayden moved to N.Y.C. in 1858. The company manufactured daguerreotype mats patented by Hiram W. Hayden (*see* Hiram Hayden, Die-engravers). Firm listed at 81 Chambers St. and 63 Reade St., N.Y.C., 1858-61.
NYA; CD; HJ

HOMER, ALFRED P. Morocco case store. Listed at 189 Chestnut St., Phila., 1848.
OPW

JAIGER AND ADAMS Morocco case manufacturer. Listed at 81 Nassau St., N.Y.C., 1856-57.
MM

KEY, FREDERICK C. & SONS Manufacturer of the plastic "Excelsior Ambrotype Case." Inventor of the "Inserted Hinge and Catch" for daguerreotype cases. See also "Biographies of Engraver-Diesinkers."

KOLT AND BLOOMHART Manufacturer of morocco and velvet cases. Listed at 8 Harmony Court, Phila., 1856-57.
MM

LEWIS, W. AND W. H. Jobbers and manufacturers of daguerreian materials and apparatus and inventors. Listed at 142 Chatham, N.Y.C., 1848-52. Listed as Premium Daguerrean Depot and Manufactory, 1851. Sold business to Messrs. Gardner, Harrison & Co., 1851-52 (?). Owner large manufacturing establishment of daguerreotype supplies located in Daguerreville, N. Y. (one mile south of Newburg, N. Y.), 1853-(?). Invented daguerreotype plate holder and issued U. S. Patent (6,819) Oct. 23, 1849; other photographic patent in 1851 (10,233).
HJ; "Scientific American; CD, NYC; RT; U. S. Patent Records.

LITTLEFIELD, PARSONS & CO. (*see* A. P. Critchlow & Co.) Manufacturer of plastic daguerreotype cases and other items of plastic composition. Successor to A. P. Critchlow & Co., Northampton, Mass. From 1858 manufactured plastic cases until the firm changed its name in 1866 to Florence Manufacturing Co. Listed also at 36 Warren St., N.Y.C., 1859; listed in both Northampton, and Florence, Mass., 1860. The company became the largest manufacturers of plastic cases in the late 1850's.
BD, NYC; NE

MARTIN, S. A. Manufacturer of daguerreotype case linings. Listed at 112 William St., N.Y.C., 1856-57.
MM

MAUSOLEUM DAGUERREOTYPE CASE CO. Manufacturer of daguerreotype cases (probably for the deceased). Listed at 335 Broadway, N.Y.C., 1856-57.
MM

MEADE BROS. Pioneer daguerreians, jobbers, manufacturers. Charles Richard Meade and brother Henry W. Meade were active in Albany, N. Y. as daguerreians, jobbers and manufacturers, and later N.Y.C. Established as first daguerreians in Albany, N. Y., 1841. Believed to have made miniature cases C. 1842. Exhibited daguerreotypes at Amer. Inst., 1846 (from Albany). Charles Meade visited Europe in 1848; took seven portraits of Daguerre. Exhibited daguerreotypes (from N.Y.C.) at Crystal Palace, London, 1851. Sold Albany establishment, Oct. 30, 1850 to Schoomaker and Morrison. Gallery in N.Y.C. and also jobber and manufacturer of daguerreotype materials, including miniature cases. Listed at 233 Broadway, N.Y.C., 1850-(?). Listed at 293

Broadway, 1858.

"Albany Daily Knickerbocker"; "American Advertiser", 1850; DJ; RT; NYA

MOFFET, J. G.   Brass rolling mill, sheet brass, German silver daguerreotype plates and mats. Listed in Bloomfield, N. J., 1850.

SBD

PEACOCK AND FICKERT   Morocco case manufacturers. Listed at 61 Walnut St., Phila., 1856-57.

MM

PECK, SAMUEL   Grocer, pioneer daguerreian, inventor, manufacturer of plastic daguerreotype cases, carver, music hall proprieter, and undertaker. Began daguerreotyping 1844 as associate with Phineas Pardee, Jr., New Haven, Conn. Took over studio in own name, Dec., 1845. Invented daguerreotype plate holder; issued patent for it April 30, 1850 (7,326). Gave up daguerreotyping, 1850. Co-partnership with Scovill Mfg. Co. for manufacturing miniature cases, New Haven, Conn., March, 1851. Associated with Ogden Hall (*see* Ogden Hall) from 1850-53. Experimented with a plastic composition, 1852; issued a U. S. Patent (11,758), Oct. 3, 1854, for daguerreotype case (plastic). In 1855 the co-partnership between Scovill Mfg. Co. and S. Peck was formalized by chartering of a joint stock company under title Samuel Peck and Co. Was issued a U. S. Patent for "fastening for the Hinges of Daguerreotype Cases," Feb. 5, 1856 (14,202). Peck's interests in the company were purchased in 1857, and Peck left the concern in that year. Samuel Peck and Co. listed as daguerreotype case manufacturer, Day St. and West Chapel, New Haven, Conn., 1851-58. Also listed at this address in 1857 was Mile Peck, "Manufacturer of Patent Stamping Machines, Power and other Presses and Oval Die Chucks." Listed as S. Peck and Co., 30 Day St., New Haven, Conn., 1858-59; Mile Peck listed at 3 Whitney Ave. In this same year Samuel Peck was listed as a Carver at 9 Atkison. Listed as Samuel Peck, P. and Alling, 6 Dwight Place (home), 1859-60. From the years 1861-76 listed as Proprietor of Music Hall. In 1876, Proprietor of Music Hall and Undertaking. In 1877-79 listed as Undertaker only. Peck was not listed in the city directories after this date.

Notes, courtesy of Dr. P. W. Bishop; CD; DJ; U. S. Patent records; information courtesy of New Haven Free Public Library

PECK, SAMUEL, JR.   Listed as daguerreotype case manufacturer at Day St., New Haven, Conn., 1853-54. Probably son of Samuel Peck.

CD

PLUMBE, JOHN, JR.   First effective advocate of railroad to Pacific, large scale promoter of photography, pioneer daguerreian, case manufacturer, inventor, author. Born Wales, July, 1809; died Dubuque, Iowa, July, 1857. Came to America age 12. By 1830 railroad surveyor in Western, Pa. Railroad superintendent, Richmond to Roanoke River, N. C., 1832. Moved Wisconsin Territory, 1836. Same year advocated railroad between Milwaukee and Sinipee, Wisconsin. Secured $2,000 Grant from Congress for railroad survey, 1838. Correspondent for leading newspapers in several American cities under name "Iowaian." Author of *Sketches of Iowa and Wisconsin,* published, 1839. Also other writings. Turned to daguerreotyping to recoup finances. Became established by 1840. Active Boston, 1841, and by 1843 had chain of photographic galleries in several cities. Patent for *Improvement in Galvanic Batteries,* 1843. Manufactured daguerreotype cases at the "Plumbe National Daguerrian Depot," N.Y.C., C. 1841-47. Hired artists to make lithographs, copied from original daguerreotypes of well known persons, which sold under name *Plumbeotypes*. Published in Phila., *National Plumbeotype Gallery,* 1847. Business failure in 1847, galleries sold to pay creditors. Continued interest in railroad to Pacific. To Iowa, then to California, 1849; next five years in California. Failed to improve finances; committed suicide Dubuque, Iowa, 1857.

"Boston Advertiser," Mar., 1841; RT; U. S. Patent records; "Sketches of Iowa and Wisconsin" (introduction), reprint by The State Historical Soc. of Iowa; "Who Was Who in America", 1963; RC (case)

ROBINSON, L.   Daguerreotype case manufacturer. Listed in Bristol. Conn., 1848.

NE

SCHLEUNES, C. C.   Manufacturer of daguerreotype cases and other articles. Listed at 25 South 2 St., Phila., 1848.

OPW

SCOTT AND WOODRUFF   Daguerreotype case manufacturers. Listed in Oxford, Conn., 1849.

NE

SCOVILL MANUFACTURING CO.   Manufacturer of metals and metal products, photographic supplies. Began business in Waterbury, Conn., about 1820 as manufacturer of buttons and trade tokens. Maintained permanent exhibition of their plated products in N.Y.C. prior to 1840. Pioneers in making daguerreotype plates. Supplied mats for miniature cases as early as 1842. Established N.Y.C. store in late summer of 1846 at 101 William St. Became interested in daguerreotype cases after 1846 (*see* Ogden Hall and Samuel Peck). Listed at 57 Maiden Lane, N.Y.C., 1850-57 and at 36 Park Row and 4 Beekman, N.Y.C., 1859. The photographic division of the company was separated from the metalworking company under the name The Scovill and Adams Company of New York, 1889. In 1901 the E. and H. T. Anthony and Co. merged with the Scovill and Adams to become Anthony and

Scovill Company which later (1907) became the Ansco Company. The Agfa Ansco corporation was formed in 1928.
Information courtesy of Edward H. Davis (Scovill Mfg. Co.); notes, courtesy of Dr. P. W. Bishop; CD, NYC; RT

SHEW, MYRON Pioneer daguerreian, miniature casemaker. Brother of Jacob, Trueman and William. Active with brother William as casemaker in Boston at 123 Washington St., 1848-49. Listed as daguerreian and jobber, casemaker, at 118 Chestnut St., Phila., 1852-57. Dealer in daguerreian and photographic goods and Morocco casemaker at same address, 1856-57.
CD, Boston; CD, Phila.; HJ; MM; RC (case)

SHEW, JACOB Pioneer daguerreian, miniature casemaker. Brother of Myron, Trueman and William. Active Baltimore, Md. Listed as J. Shew's Daguerreian Gallery at 117 Baltimore St., Baltimore, Md., 1853. To San Francisco, 1854.
CD; RC (case)

SHEW, WILLIAM Pioneer daguerreian, miniature casemaker. Brother of Jacob, Myron, and Trueman. Active Boston during 1840's. Listed as casemaker at 60½ Cornhill, Boston, Mass., 1844; 16 Haskins Blg., 1845-48; 123 Washington St., 1848-50. Not listed in 1850 as casemaker; to Calif. in this year. Sold business to John Sawyer in 1851; the new name was New England Daguerreotype Stock Depot. Took panoramic view of San Francisco, C. 1852. Continued to be active in San Francisco as photographer.
CD; NE; DJ (1851); RC (case and photographs)

SIMONS, M. P. (*see* Simons & Willis, N. A. Simons, Simons & Wight) Pioneer daguerreian, miniature casemaker, author. Listed in Phila. as merchant, 1841. Occupation as gas fitter at 173 Chestnut St., 1842. Listed case manufacturer, same address, 1843. Listed as case manufacturer at 100 Chestnut St., 1844-48. After 1848 listed as daguerreian only at 179 Chestnut St. Assigned U. S. Patent (3,085) for coloring daguerreotypes from Warren Thompson, 1843. Wrote books on photography subjects, 1857-60.
CD; Root, 1864

SIMONS, NOAH A. (*see* M. P. Simons) Box manufacturer and miniature casemaker. Listed as box manufacturer at 20 S. 4th St., Phila., 1846; listed at 179 Chestnut St., Phila., 1848.
CD

SIMONS & WILLIS (*see* M. P. Simons and Noah A. Simons) Miniature case manufacturers. Listed at 173 Chestnut St., Phila., 1843.
CD

SIMONS & WIGHT (*see* M. P. Simons) Manufacturer of Morocco work of all description—jewelry, dental, surgical, dissecting, music cases and daguerreotype cases. Listed at 20 S. 4th St., Phila., 1846.
OPW

SMITH, FREDERICK, H. Manufacturer and dealer in pocketbooks, Morocco cases including miniature cases. Listed at 97 Chestnut St., Phila., 1846; 52½ Chestnut St., Phila., 1848.
OPW, 1846, 1848

SMITH, GEORGE Brooklyn (N.Y.) daguerreotype cover manufacturer; res., 240 Navy.

SMITH, J. H. Miniature casemaker. Active Boston, 1845. Made case covered with goatskin which sold for $17.00.
Beaumont Newhall, "The Daguerreotype in America," 1961

SMITH, J. R. Morocco case manufacturer. Listed at 23 Ferry St., N.Y.C., 1853.
CSP

SNYDER, F. W. Manufacturer of Morocco, jewelry, and miniature cases, N.Y.C., 1858.
NYA

STUDLEY, HIRAM Miniature casemaker. First listed at 16 Haskins Bldg. (corner Court and Howard), Boston, Mass., 1848-50.
BD

STUDLEY AND GORDON Miniature case manufacturer. Listed at 5 Hanover St., Boston, Mass., C. 1846. Business known as "Miniature Case Manufactory."
RC (case)

TAYLOR, EDWARD G. Daguerreotype case manufacturer. Listed at 128 Fulton and 89 Nassau St., N.Y.C., 1850.
"American Advertiser," 1850

WADHAM'S MANUFACTURING CO. Manufacturer of plastic daguerreotype cases featuring the Kinsley & Parker Hinge.
Coll. of Janie Wright

WEBBER, J. Morocco case manufacturer. Listed at 5 North William St., N.Y.C., 1856-57.
MM

WHITE, EDWARD Pioneer daguerreian, jobber and manufacturer of photographic materials including daguerreotype cases. Active N.Y.C. as early as 1842. Manufactured daguerreotype plates, 1844. Listed at 178 Broadway, N.Y.C., 1845-47; 175 Broadway, 1847-49, and at 247 Broadway, 1849-50.

Notes, courtesy of Dr. P. W. Bishop; "Scientific American; BD; Root, 1864

WILLARD, J. W. AND CO. Hardware store, photographic supplies. Listed at 118 William St., N.Y.C., 1859; 522 Broadway, N.Y.C., off St. Nicholas Hotel, 1860. Put advertising label in plastic daguerreotype case. Known as fashionable store, mostly retail.

BD, NYC, 1859; "The American Journal of Photography," 1860; Coll. of Mrs. Janie Wright (case)

Biographies of Die-engravers

GASKILL AND COPPER   John C. Copper was listed as an engraver in Phila., 1839-60. In 1850 living in Spring Garden Ward, Phila., Pa. Signed name Gaskill and Copper appears on paper-covered miniature case, C. 1858.
NYHS; CD; RC (case)

GOLL, FREDERICK P. (GALL)   Diesinker, engraver, and letter cutter. Also listed as daguerreotype casemaker. Born Germany. First listed in directory at 112 Fulton St., N.Y.C., 1841-46 and later at 78 Fulton St., N.Y.C., 1847-60. Worked for Library of American History, Cincinnati, O., C. 1851. A diemaker for Samuel Peck and Company (H. Halvorson and S. Peck patent), 1854-60 (?). Reproduced in dies, *The Capture of Major André* from a painting by Asher B. Durand; *The Washington Monument*, Richmond, Va.; a medallion of George Washington; a horse race; *The Launching*.
NYHS; CD, NYC; RC

HAYDEN, HIRAM W.   Diemaker, embosser, inventor, and daguerreian. Worked for Scovill Manufacturing Co., before 1854 as diemaker and embosser. Was called the "artist of the village," Waterbury, Conn., 1851; produced three daguerreotype scenes on paper exhibited in Waterbury, 1851. Connected with Holmes, Booth and Hayden, makers of daguerreotype materials in Waterbury, Conn., and N.Y.C., 1854-58. Holder of Design Patent (733) issued Oct. 9, 1855 (ornamental mats for daguerreotype cases). Made dies for plastic daguerreotype case based on the painting, *The Calmady Children* by Sir Thomas Lawrence.
"Scientific American" (1851); CD, NYC; Notes, courtesy of Dr. P. W. Bishop.

HENNING, A.   Engraver and diesinker. Hartford, Conn., 1855-56. Listed at 29 North William St., N.Y.C., 1859-60, with Henning & Eymann, daguerreotype casemakers.
CD, Hartford, Conn., 1855-56; CD, NYC, 1859; BD, NYC, 1860; Mc-Clinton, "Handbook of Popular Antiques."

HOUSTON, W. E.   Diesinker. Designed dies for Holmes, Booth and Hayden. The only diemaker known to sign name on inside of die. His background is unknown.
RC (cases)

KEY, FREDERICK, C.   Engraver, diesinker and seal engraver. Was engraver at 27 Beekman St., N.Y.C., 1844-(?)-49; moved to Phila., 1850-55. Formed F. C. Key and Sons, diesinkers, at 123 Arch St., Phila., 1856-(?). Made dies for Samuel Peck and Co., 1854-60(?) and Scovill Manufacturing Co., about 1860-(?).
NYHS; BD, NYC; CD, Phila.

LOEKLE, CHARLES   Seal engraver. Signed leather-embossed miniature case cover design, C. Loekle, Phila. (C. 1855). Seal engraver, N.Y.C., 1858-60.
NYHS; RC (case)

PAINE, R.   Engraver and diesinker. Active Springfield, Mass., 1850's. Possibly designed first successful die for plastic cases (see *The Memorial*, Plate 62). Die was made for Samuel Peck and probably designed for images of the deceased; it is the only plastic case known to be signed by him.
Notes, courtesy of Dr. P. W. Bishop; RC (case)

PAQUET, ANTHONY C. Born Hamburg, Germany, 1814; died Phila., 1882. Engraver on wood, copper, and steel. Came to America 1848. Worked in Phila. from 1850-55; signed his name on embossed silk-covered miniature case design, Phila., C. 1852. Active N.Y.C., 1856-58. Returned Phila., assistant engraver at U. S Mint from 1857-64, and engraved the first Congressional Medal of Honor. Exhibited medals at the Pa. Acad., during the Civil War.
NYHS; RC (case)

PRETLOVE, DAVID Engraver, diesinker, and letter cutter. First listed at 241 Cherry St., N.Y.C., 1844-47, and at 78 Fulton St., (probably partner of F. Goll), 1848-50. Exhibited engravings, Amer. Inst., Oct., 1846. Signed name to several embossed designs for leather-covered miniature cases.
CD, NYC; BD, NYC; Amer. Inst. Cat., 1846-47; RC (cases)

SCHAEFER, ANTHONY Engraver and diesinker. Listed at 83 Duane St., N.Y.C., 1857-59. Made dies for Littlefield, Parsons & Co. (successors to A. P. Critchlow & Co.), 1858-(?). Mostly made historical themes.
BD, NYC; RC (cases)

SEILER, FREDERICK Engraver and diesinker. Listed in 1849 at 57 Gold St., N.Y.C.; Seiler and Rupp (Christian Rupp), 1850. Active 1850-54, N.Y.C.
NYHS; McClinton, "Handbook of Popular Antiques."

SMITH AND HARTMANN (Frederick B. Smith and Hermann Hartmann) Metal engravers and diesinkers, letter cutters. Listed N.Y.C. at 122½ Fulton St., 1850-59. Made dies for S. Peck and Co., Littlefield, Parsons & Co. Designs for plastic cases included reproducing *Washington Crossing the Delaware,* a painting by Emanuel Leutze; a painting *The Landing of Columbus* by John Vanderlyn; a country dance.
BD, NYC; NYHS

SMITH, J. Engraver and diesinker. Worked for S. Peck and Co. and other plastic case manufacturers, C. 1855-60(?). Usually depicted nature, portrait, or conventional designs. Signed name to several dies.
McClinton, "Handbook of Popular Antiques"; RC (cases)

TRUE, BENJAMIN C. Engraver, seal engraver, and diesinker. Signed design on leather-covered case C. 1842 made for Meade Bros., pioneer daguerreians and manufacturer-dealers in photographic materials, Albany, N. Y. Signature on case design reads B. C. True, Albany. Listed Cincinnati, O., 1850-60.
NYHS; RC (case)

Bibliography

American Journal Of Photography and the Allied Arts and Sciences, Seeley and Garbanti, New York, Vols. 1–9 (1858–1867).

Baring-Gould, William S. and Ceil, *The Annotated Mother Goose,* Clarkson N. Potter, Inc., New York, 1962.

Boger, Louise and H. Batterson, *The Dictionary of Antiques and the Decorative Arts,* Charles Scribner's Sons, New York, 1957.

Cirlot, J. E., *A Dictionary of Symbols,* Philosophical Library, New York, 1962.

Daguerreian Journal, The. New York: 1850–1851. Title changed to *Humphrey's Journal.* New York: 1852–1862.

DuBois, J. H. and F. W. John. *Plastics.* New York: Reinhold Publishing Company, 1967.

Fairholt, F. W. *A Dictionary of Terms in Art.* London: Virtue, Hall and Virtue, 1854.

Ferguson, George. *Signs and Symbols in Christian Art,* New York: Oxford University Press, 1954.

Groce, George C. and Wallace, David H. *The New York Historical Society's Dictionary of Artists in America 1564–1860,* New Haven: Yale University Press, 1957.

Kitson, Michael. *The Age of Baroque.* New York: McGraw-Hill, 1966.

Larkin, Oliver W. *Art and Life in America.* New York: Holt, Rinehart and Winston, 1960.

Lawler, P. J. *Embossing.* Malden, Massachusetts: 1891.

Lehner, Ernst and Johanna. *Folklore and Symbolism of Flowers, Plants and Trees.* New York: Tudor Publishing Company, 1960.

Lynes, Russell. *The Tastemakers.* New York: Harper and Brothers, 1954.

McClinton, Katherine. *Handbook of Popular Antiques.* New York: Random House, 1946.

National Academy of Design Exhibition Records 1826–1860. New York Historical Society. Vols. 1–2: 1943.

Newhall, Beaumont. *The Daguerreotype in America.* New York: Duell, Sloan and Pearce, 1961.

Plastic Institute Transactions. London: October, 1961.

Reynolds, Graham. *English Portrait Miniatures.* London: Adam and Charles Black, 1952.

Rinhart, Floyd and Marion. *American Daguerreian Art.* New York: Clarkson N. Potter, Inc., 1967.

———. "An American Way of Death," *Art in America,* Vol. 55, No. 5 (1967), 78–81.

———. "America's Forgotten Folding Stereoscope Case," *The Antiques Journal,* Vol. 23, No. 6 (June, 1968), 12–13.

Root, Marcus A. *The Camera and the Pencil.* New York: 1864.

Shaw, Henry. *The Decorative Arts- Ecclesiastical and Civil of the Middle Ages.* London: William Pickering, 1851.

Snelling, Henry Hunt. *A Dictionary of the Photographic Art.* New York: 1854.

Taft, Robert. *Photography and the American Scene.* New York: The Macmillan Company, 1938.

Ward, James. *Historic Ornament, Treatise on Decorative Art and Architectual Ornament.* London: Chapman and Hall Ltd., 1897, 1909.

Index